T0311602

Cambridge Elements ≡

Elements in Public Policy
edited by
M. Ramesh
National University of Singapore (NUS)
Michael Howlett
Simon Fraser University, British Colombia
Xun WU
Hong Kong University of Science and Technology
Judith Clifton
University of Cantabria
Eduardo Araral
National University of Singapore (NUS)

HERDING SCIENTISTS

A Story of Failed Reform at the CDC

Andrew B. Whitford
University of Georgia

CAMBRIDGE
UNIVERSITY PRESS

University Printing House, Cambridge CB2 8BS, United Kingdom

One Liberty Plaza, 20th Floor, New York, NY 10006, USA

477 Williamstown Road, Port Melbourne, VIC 3207, Australia

314–321, 3rd Floor, Plot 3, Splendor Forum, Jasola District Centre,
New Delhi – 110025, India

103 Penang Road, #05–06/07, Visioncrest Commercial, Singapore 238467

Cambridge University Press is part of the University of Cambridge.

It furthers the University's mission by disseminating knowledge in the pursuit of
education, learning, and research at the highest international levels of excellence.

www.cambridge.org
Information on this title: www.cambridge.org/9781108824101
DOI: 10.1017/9781108915175

First published 2022

A catalogue record for this publication is available from the British Library.

ISBN 978-1-108-82410-1 Paperback
ISSN 2398-4058 (online)
ISSN 2514-3565 (print)

Herding Scientists

A Story of Failed Reform at the CDC

Elements in Public Policy

DOI: 10.1017/9781108915175
First published online: April 2022

Andrew B. Whitford
University of Georgia

Author for correspondence: Andrew B. Whitford, aw@uga.edu

Abstract: When politicians reshape public health agencies, scientists resist changes and, if possible, leave. Those shifts make it harder for agencies to fight future public health threats. This Element focuses on the tension between scientists and managerial control in the policy process, both conceptually and empirically. It centers on a failed attempt to reorganize the US Centers for Disease Control and Prevention. Because many of the gains in longevity and health quality result from the work of public health agencies, public health scientists and practitioners are the frontline producers of public health.

Keywords: public health, scientists, reorganization, politics, innovation

ISBNs: 9781108824101 (PB), 9781108915175 (OC)
ISSNs: 2398-4058 (online), 2514-3565 (print)

Contents

1 Introduction

How do we decide what public health is? What are the consequences of those decisions? International, national, state, and local decisions by governments, firms, and nongovernmental actors combine to help determine the "public" part of public health. These actors come together for many purposes (e.g., assessment, monitoring, evaluation, planning). But the objectives they choose are not meaningless: public agencies are charged with delivering and insuring those population-level public health outcomes.

For instance, in 1988, the United States Institute of Medicine (IOM) 1988 report *The Future of Public Health* indicted the American public health system as a dizzyingly complex, disjointed array of governmental bodies and programs (United States Institute of Medicine, 1988). For the IOM, public health objectives should depend on scientific/technical knowledge, public values, and popular opinions. Agencies, policymakers, and the public should work together to prioritize health goals and services; once determined, agencies should assure the community that they could meet those goals.

Yet the debate continued about what was necessary to improve the American public health system. Some highlighted the need for reform and increased capacity (Baker et al., 1994), while others focused on the importance of local public health agencies (Milne, 2000). Specific topics, such as responding to bioterrorism, made their way to the public agenda (Baker & Koplan, 2002). Later IOM reports shifted attention from public agencies to the ecosystem of nongovernmental actors (United States Institute of Medicine, 2003). One broad theme was strengthening the system to make it more effective, community-based, and collaborative (Berkowitz et al., 2005), but more specific topics on the agenda included terrorism preparedness and response, America's aging population, obesity's health consequences, globalization and new infectious diseases, and the need to modernize the public health workforce and infrastructure. These changes in the policy agenda brought about a range of policy proposals – and these proposals spurred politicians and agencies to act.

Shaping Policy through Agency Design

In polities, one way such debates about public values are expressed is through broadscale attempts to "reform" the system through reorganization (Hanson et al., 1974; March et al., 1993; Peters, 1992). Those structural debates often center on the roles scientists play in the overall policy process. In recent years, such debates also have brought public attention to the interaction of politics and professionalism in the organizations we charge with designing and implementing policies about complex issues like climate change, agricultural research, criminal prosecution, and national security. Throughout the years and in each of these arenas, we have seen clearly how politics and other pressures shape the relative power and position of professionals like scientists, engineers, lawyers, and economists (e.g., Bowen, 2008; Wilkinson, 1998).

Governments depend on professionals like scientists to help improve policy outcomes, but scientists are just one part of complex policy processes. Scholars of policy, agencies, and reorganization have considered the roles of scientists in the policy process and complex organizations for quite some time. Yet, few examine the intersection of these topics. Research innovations like the advocacy coalition framework have centered our attention on scientists, and our knowledge of policy processes is richer because of those innovations. For instance, we know scientists are core to understanding advocacy coalitions (Sabatier, 1988; Weible & Sabatier, 2009), and we know that the role of evidence in policy processes has changed over time (Howlett, 2009; Majone, 1989).

We know much less about how organizational pressures affect scientists in complex public organizations like national federal agencies in the US. While the literature on "managing scientists" is rich with cases from the private sector, universities, and hospitals, we know less about those processes when the organization is situated in national political settings that shape organizational missions and expectations about behavior. A broad array of literature focuses on managing professionals (like doctors) in small-scale settings (Buchanan et al., 2007; Currie et al., 2012; Davies, 2003; Forbes et al., 2004; Hunter, 1992), but few address managing scientists in large-scale national public organizations like federal agencies (Crow & Bozeman, 1998).

Researchers in both political science and public administration have argued that political actors seek to refocus the attention of or change behavior within complex public agencies to achieve broader political and policy goals. For instance, Terry Moe has focused on reorganization as a tool for shaping policy processes in institutions (Moe, 1989). Yet, while reorganization and structural changes in firms and universities are well understood, we know less empirically about reorganization dynamics in the public sector (Boyle, 1979; Christensen & Lægreid, 2007; Lee et al., 2020; Maynard-Moody et al., 1986; Peters, 1992; Pfiffner, 2007; Rainey & Thompson, 2006; Thomas, 1993; Whitford, 2020). Moreover, we know little about those dynamics when the targets of those processes are organizations populated by scientists.

The main purpose of this Element is to help fill a gap in our understanding of complex policy processes – our lack of attention to the tension between scientists and managerial control in the policy process, both conceptually and empirically. The Element offers a unique perspective on this understudied aspect of the policy process – the ways in which politicians and agency leaders attempt to "herd" or direct scientists through the reshaping of public agencies. At a conceptual level, this discussion is part of broader movements to understand the impact of the professions in policy processes. This is because professions both enable policy improvements and limit the ability of political overseers to reshape organizations.

At a more practical level, this Element centers on a failed reorganization attempt. Unlike in the private sector, where bankruptcy proceedings of Chapter 11 of the United States Bankruptcy Code create ample opportunities to study the "dog that didn't bark" (the company that did not successfully reorganize), most reform attempts in the public sector are cast as "successes" by those who attempt them – regardless of their impacts. Indeed, it is difficult to discover the consequences of even "successful" reorganizations (March & Olson, 1983); as Salamon at one time argued, "serious empirical work on the real effects of reorganization is not only deficient, it is non-existent" (Salamon, 1981, 60). This is a practical concern if only in that each future reform attempt is in some ways a response to a past failure to reform the organization – what happens next depends on what did not happen in the past (Sinclair & Whitford, 2013; Sydow et al., 2009; Whetten, 1987).

Reorganizing Public Health Science

Broadly speaking, numerous countries have sought to answer the previously posed questions. Specifically, the US used a deliberative goal-setting process to set national public health goals, and that process fed attempts to reform the primary agency charged with administering public health science. In a nutshell, as new public problems like anthrax (Decker, 2018), severe acute respiratory syndrome (SARS), and other infectious diseases emerged in the 2000s, the US and other countries all moved to reorganize public health scientific capacity. To examine how such deliberations play out in one agency, I offer a narrative drawn from the most important attempt to reorganize the US Centers for Disease Control and Prevention (CDC) since World War II (Etheridge, 1992).

CDC's leaders, staff, and partners sought to answer the question "what is public health?" through strategic visioning; leaders then chose an organizational model drawn from business consulting that had largely been abandoned in the private sector. The changes this model dictated – and the way in which leaders tried to implement the change process – created turmoil and led to the departures of key scientists and managers.

On April 21, 2005, Dr. Julie Gerberding, Director of the CDC, announced that the CDC had "taken a landmark step in its readiness to confront the challenges of 21st-century health threats" (US Centers for Disease Control and Prevention, 2005, 1). The process of reorganization began in 2003 and involved two years of detailed collaboration inside the agency with line and staff and outside the agency with a broad array of stakeholders, culminating in the 2005 unveiling of the full plan.

The mission of "the new CDC" was "to promote health and quality of life by preventing and controlling disease, injury, and disability" by working with a variety of partners, located in the United States and throughout the world, to accomplish specific goals. This included monitoring health and health problems, conducting research and developing policies, implementing strategies that help people select healthy behaviors, developing future generations of leadership, and training health professionals for solving emerging problems.

To accomplish these goals, the "Futures Initiative" called for reducing the number of Gerberding's direct reports from twenty-three to thirteen by creating six overarching "Coordinating Centers." The Coordinating Centers represented a switch in tactics to make the CDC more flexible and responsive. Common themes in the Futures Initiative were greater coordination across the key components of the CDC, improving the impact of CDC activities in terms of American health, increasing accountability (especially in terms of business services), and building on a well-developed network of relationships to expand partnerships in the areas of science, services, and administration.

The CDC has long been considered an agency of "virus hunters" (McCormick et al., 1999); we know less about its organizational life as a public health science agency. The vignette of the CDC offered here represents important grounding for theories of change in agencies populated by scientists. It helps us better understand how science agencies like the CDC try to harness the input and support of stakeholders and partners. This is notable because the broader context shows that this reorganization attempt to reenvision public health had much in common with that of other countries in terms of purposes, processes, and timing regarding responses to key public health challenges. Moreover, that process sought to change the agency from a traditional hierarchy long marked by organizational "silos" to a new matrix structure, enhancing organizational flexibility and information sharing. Extensive deliberation among stakeholders over the organization's goals precipitated the choice of a novel matrix structure for increased effectiveness. However, those choices carried costs associated with this form of organizational goal setting and changes to top leadership, line staff, and the broader public health community, as reflected in operations and human capital effects.

By 2009, new leaders had already started to roll back all the changes of the Futures Initiative. In a short time, nothing of consequence remained of those changes, and the CDC was already on a new reform path. The buildings remained, and the agency's structure was closer to its old one, but many senior scientists were gone. The Futures Initiative was a failed reform. It unraveled so quickly that we cannot assess its effects on the agency – except by assessing the change process itself. There is no "post" experiment to compare to the "pre." Long on design, it fell short on implementation.

This Element examines this narrative about the CDC to help us better understand how political motives, organizational theories, public problems, and scientific professionalism become entwined in public health. Most of the gains in longevity and health quality have resulted from the work of organizations like the CDC, making public health scientists and practitioners the front-line producers of health.

Yet herding scientists is fraught with risk, and governing scientific organizations is a less-understood aspect of traditional policy implementation. To help improve this understanding, I focus on four messages. First, the Element draws the "big picture" within which this story proceeds: new public problems emerge, politicians and their proxies demand change, and professionals like scientists seek and advocate for solutions. "Herding scientists" is a core part of the policy process. Second, political appointees attempt to "steer the boat" of public scientific organizations through tools like reorganization, but reorganization is not a singular event; it is a policy process involving constituencies, stakeholders, and sellers of advice. Third, reorganization and reform have consequences for how agencies do their daily work in deciding what to do and how to do it. In this way, the reorganization attempt may be the big policy battle, but the process is really a multitude of smaller skirmishes – none of which occurs in a vacuum and without its own history. Fourth, scientists live inside agencies, but few joined to implement organizational change. Consequently, in the CDC, morale suffered greatly, and many valuable public health scientists left the organization.

This Element centers on a dilemma: the outcomes of many policy processes depend on the knowledge and technical expertise of scientists, but most of the agencies they reside in are managed by generalists appointed by politicians. One of the most potent methods for "shuffling the deck" and changing those outcomes is reorganizing the agency's groups of scientists – most of whom are disinterested in organizational change. How does that dynamic play out? In several ways, the Element builds a grounded theory about these and related dynamics.

My main point remains on the dynamics that define the reform of complex agencies like the CDC – on how herding scientists is itself a policy process. After building a theory, this Element reviews the broader public health context before offering a deep discussion of reorganization attempts at the CDC, the motives behind them, the methods and participation models used, the role of leaders and their motives, the reorganization models selected and their origins in business, and the consequences of these factors in the context of the CDC as a science-based organization. I pay special attention to the presentation of empirical evidence drawn from surveys about these consequences.

After this deep discussion, I draw several broad conclusions about the roles of politics, leadership, and ideas in the context of the main dilemma: How do organizations like the CDC balance science and managerial control in complex policymaking environments? Finally, in the conclusion, I offer a short discussion of this exercise for our improved understanding of complex policy processes. As noted, there are any number of ways in which similar dynamics are playing out or soon will play out – with attendant consequences for policy selection and implementation.

The Value of This Story

The world's recent experiences in the coronavirus pandemic will lead to calls to reform our global public health systems. In the conclusion, I describe why this is probably inevitable, but recent books like Andy Slavitt's *Preventable: The Inside Story of How Leadership Failures, Politics, and Selfishness Doomed the U.S. Coronavirus Response* (Slavitt, 2021), Scott Gottlieb's *Uncontrolled Spread: Why COVID-19 Defeated Us and How We Can Beat the Next Pandemic* (Gottlieb, 2021), and Michael Lewis' *The Premonition: A Pandemic Story* (Lewis, 2021) all signal that there is money to be made in calls for reform and change. The point of the story I document here is that we have been down this road before. After the anthrax events and the 9/11 attack, we tried to reorganize our way to policy change at the CDC – and it failed. There are rarely "silver bullet" solutions to changing agencies, but perhaps this story helps us better understand the complex world of herding scientists.

2 Scientists, Managerial Control, and Reform

Professionals act as a fulcrum in this political game of shaping public organizations. As new problems emerge and the public and the politicians who represent them come to demand change, professionals (often scientists) are asked to determine what is needed and how to achieve improvement in social conditions. While political appointees are the mechanism through which politicians seek to shape those public scientific organizations, appointees wield tools (like reorganization) that are only coarse mechanisms for redirecting how scientists go about doing the public's business. This is partly because reorganization is itself a policy process involving constituencies, stakeholders, and sellers of advice.

Redirecting scientists means using reorganization to change how agencies decide what to do and how to do it. Reorganization involves changing low-level activities within organizations that professionals engage with daily – the organization's rules, routines, and procedures. Yet, scientists as professionals are relatively unique in that few join those organizations because of natural inclinations toward management or organizational "tending" (the hard work of healing and redirecting fractured organizations; Powley & Piderit, 2008). As in other organizations, such discordances naturally lead to "exit, voice, and loyalty" problems (Hirschman, 1970; Lee & Whitford, 2007; Whitford & Lee, 2015).

This section first turns to scientists as professionals and their lives in organizations that depend on their expertise, for it is the scientists who play the central role in the CDC narrative offered in Section 3. I then offer a broad view of reorganization and what often changes in terms of day-to-day operations. After that, given the nature of the changes discussed in the CDC as a public health science organization, I then discuss the origin of those changes in the business literature. Finally, given this viewpoint, I offer a brief overview of the reorganization literature with a focus on politicians shaping agency design.

Administrative Rituals and Science Professionals

Debates over the true nature of administrative reorganization in public agencies should start with a synthetic discussion of the bureaucrats themselves – for it is their production and activities that are the ultimate focus of all reorganization attempts. In this section, my focus is on professionals, scientists as professionals, and scientists operating in a world of administrative rituals (March & Olson, 1983).

First, scholars largely agree about what constitutes a profession and what those aspects bring to our understanding of the day-to-day operations of professionals in organizations (Freidson, 2001; Hall, 1968; Miller & Whitford, 2016; Wilensky, 1964). Professions are centered on bodies of knowledge that create wells of expertise for their operators. Professionals have surprisingly long-term career perspectives and often self-identify with their profession for longer than they serve in a specific organization. Professionals operate themselves in relative insulation and exercise relative oversight of their members and the bodies of knowledge they curate. Finally, professionals have had long-standing relative independence from sources of authority centered in hierarchies – that in fact part of professionalism is the maintenance of "elaborate social arrangements, formal and information, [to] sustain this autonomy" (Wilensky, 1964, 146).

These aspects stand in contrast to the relative position of managers and the administrative rituals they curate because managerialism "denies authority to expertise by claiming a form of general knowledge that is superior to specialization and because it can organize it rationally and efficiently" (Freidson, 2001, 117). For political scientists, these functions of professionalism create opportunities for political credible commitment to specific policy paths (Miller & Whitford, 2016). As Moe (1987) notes: "Professionals are difficult to control, but their behavior is fairly easy to predict. And that, of course, is at the heart of all this. A professional, if given total autonomy and insulated from external pressures, can be counted upon to behave in a manner characteristic of his type. That is what true professionalism is all about. (259)"

But political scientists also recognize that these attributes make professionals inherently undependable (in political terms) because they are difficult to recruit and retain (Gailmard & Patty, 2007). In sum, professionals are important components in a theory of political reshaping of agencies, and proceeding without their consideration is a futile exercise.

Second, scientists are a unique brand of professionals that warrant special consideration and treatment – indeed, scientists can be considered the "profession par excellence according to [Talcott] Parsons" (Brante, 1988, 119; Parsons, 1939). Since the beginning of modern science, academics have struggled to characterize scientists' mental models, purposes, organization, and utility within broader society and its institutions (Meier, 1951; Merton, 1957; Tarkowski & Turnbull, 1959). Indeed, much of our understanding of the professions as a social construct relies on our understanding of the unique role of scientists in society (Carr-Saunders & Wilson, 1933). The attributes of professions laid out here are even more important in considering the special role of scientists – if only because we have long recognized that "the most important goal for the 'typical' scientist is that of advancing the knowledge of his field by some form of basic research" (Glaser, 1964, 1). While our understanding of scientists' mental models, purposes, and other aspects has certainly evolved over time, it is impossible to discuss scientists within agencies without that starting assumption: that they develop, curate, and maintain bodies of knowledge that exist outside the bounds of public agencies.

Within the policy process literature, though, we have come to understand similarly important roles in the evolution of policy debates, adjudication of policy knowledge, and even the advocacy of specific policy positions (Sabatier, 1988; Smith, 1992; Weible & Sabatier, 2009). We also know the complexity of the process by which scientific knowledge and evidence is translated into policy

(Howlett, 2009; Majone, 1989), but such understandings do not tell us that scientists are just like other actors in the policy process – indeed, they are a reminder of the long recognition that scientists are different, that they see themselves as different, and perhaps even that they should be different. There are benefits in the predictability of being a special type.

These aspects of science as a profession create special concerns when it comes to their management. Long recognized in the literature on professions, scientists and administrators rarely share a mutual understanding of what are the organizational problems and how they should be solved. Even sixty years ago, the clash between scientists and managers was seen as being fundamental to the organization's operations: that "it is well known that professional scientists and professional administrators often lack sympathy for each other's point of view," so "the results may vary from lack of co-operation, due to absence of interest or understanding, to occasional open clashes" (Tarkowski & Turnbull, 1959, 213–214). From that point, researchers have sought to better understand those problems and their possible solutions.

Yet, little of that research literature speaks to the problem of managing scientists working in public organizations, even though we have long recognized that the problems may be greatest in those settings (Tarkowski & Turnbull, 1959, 214). This is especially interesting given the role of science in large government institutions throughout World War II and during the Cold War (Carpenter, 2001, 2010). Most of what has been written comes from the point of view of how to manage scientists and engineers in generic firms and similar organizations (Badawy, 1995; Glaser, 1964; Kerr et al., 1977; Raelin, 1991; Sapienza, 2004; Sayles & Chandler, 1971). Most of that literature simply argues for applying lessons from traditional management theory to the domain of scientists.

In contrast, in their seminal study of the US federal research and development (R&D) laboratories, Crow and Bozeman (1998) lay out a synthetic, developmental understanding of the way such organizations evolve and perform in a public sector setting. While their broader focus is on an empirical understanding of their operations (for instance, helping continue their understanding of "red tape" in knowledge organizations), they also help us understand a major point about those organizations: that "public policies affecting R&D laboratories seem to pay little heed to the laboratories themselves . . . that politics pay so little heed to the character and quality of their instrument [for solving public problems]" (p. xx).

This Element adds to this lineage by turning the question of the management of scientists in government on its side: rather than focusing on the political redesign of public organizations populated by bland bureaucrats, in the narrative that follows, the public organization is populated by scientists. Instead of concentrating on the general management of scientists, this narrative centers on a public agency that politicians seek to reshape and redesign. In the words of Crow and Bozeman (1998), the "character and quality" of the CDC is a core part of processes that seek to shape its policy outputs through reorganization. While reorganization often takes the form of "administrative ritual," its practical impact as a mechanism for "herding scientists" for public purposes is worth greater attention in the policy and administrative literatures.

What Reorganization Changes

Reorganization is one of the basic facts of organizational life (Gortner et al., 1997, 91). For Emmerich, reorganization is any change in executive functions that measurably affects how executive branch leaders supervise and direct how functions are exercised (Emmerich 1971, 8). In theory, the principal goals of reorganization are divided among (1) those having to do with changing policy and program; (2) those intended to improve administrative effectiveness in carrying out existing responsibilities; (3) those directed specifically to problems of personnel, individuals, or groups; and (4) those intended to counter or respond to pressures and threats from outside the organization (Mosher, 1967, 497). Peters (1992) classifies these motives as "purposive" (the intentional seeking of attaining goals), "environmental dependency" (reactions to outside changes, such as technological change), and "institutional" (maintenance of internal systems with the organization's history and values).

In practice, reorganizing the executive branch is a popular exercise, mainly because of structural fragmentation and the political independence of many bureaucracies (Meier, 1980), so reorganization is often intended to consolidate agencies to enhance control and coordination (Goodsell, 2004). Reorganization is often a tool for responding to changing priorities that assumes that centralization improves operational efficiency and effectiveness (Radin, 2007). Most modern presidents have supported some kind of organizational shuffling to reduce perceived conflict and enhance coordination (Kettl, 2021).

Yet, it is difficult to assess whether reorganization achieves its goals; some argue that perhaps "reorganization cannot attain its manifest goal" (Meier, 1980, 399). While reorganizations intend to change what agencies do (Wilson, 1989), the empirical evidence of effects is mixed at best (Lee et al., 2020; Thomas, 1993). For example, while the "semi-merger" of the Federal Bureau of Investigation and Drug Enforcement Administration in 1968 and 1973 offered new resources and redefined core tasks (Wilson, 1989, 267), "assembling a variety of agencies together into a Department of

Health, Education, and Welfare made little difference: the component bureaus ... continued for the most part to operate independently of each other and of HEW's central leadership" (Wilson, 1989, 267–268). Yet, "reorganizations [can lead] to some changes but not others; nor [are] all of the shifts necessarily desirable . . . . Its consequences [depend] on a wide range of factors, only some of which could be manipulated by policymakers or agency officials" (Hult, 1987, 6). One broad reason for this is that every reorganization is a mixture of two timelines – the first influenced by mechanisms of political attention and involvement and the second driven by long-run evolutionary processes centered around meaning and interpretation (March & Olson, 1983).

For CDC's story, addressing the impact of reorganization on an agency's scientists requires a conceptual framework that focuses on public health agencies as organizations, so the discussion here will be guided by a combination of three core theoretical frameworks centering on strategic leadership, goal setting through deliberation, and the manipulation of organizational routines. In his 1962 classic *Strategy and Structure*, Alfred Chandler argued that an organization's structure should flow from its strategy, that its structure would largely determine what the organization does, and that in turn the organization's conduct determines its overall performance (Chandler, 1990); structure links the strategy of leaders and the conduct of lower-level employees. Essentially, for organizations to change, the strategic purpose of goal setting – carried out through deliberation – is to transform the routines and rules that guide day-to-day choices in complex organizations.

How do organizations change? First, studies of organizational change have long held that *strategic action* by an organization's leaders is a primary source of change (March et al., 1993), although studies are not uniform in their assessment of how and when change can occur (Armenakis & Bedeian, 1999). For some, the ability to enact change is the definition of leadership (Yukl et al., 2002), and in fact, the public sector is replete with examples of the critical role managers play in change efforts (Fernandez & Rainey, 2006; Robertson & Seneviratne, 1995). Of course, these strategic efforts may be subject to limits (environmental, cognitive, or resource-based; Cyert & March, 1992), but their functional purpose is still to move an organization closer to its goals. Building an understanding of organizational change on strategic action (or *agency*) emphasizes how leaders construct causal chains – how they plan change processes, build internal and external support, establish support coalitions within top management, and allocate resources for the change, as well as continue to institutionalize the change (Fernandez & Rainey, 2006).

Second, scholars widely recognize the fundamental role *goal setting* plays in the overall direction of organizations (Perrow, 1961; Simon, 1964; Thompson & McEwen, 1958), as well as on the direction and commitment of individual members of organizations (Latham & Yukl, 1975; Locke et al., 1988). Research suggests that participation in goal-setting processes increases the likelihood of goal attainment, organizational performance, and satisfaction (Wagner et al., 1997). One reason participation can be beneficial is the knowledge participants hold – information that is not also held by an organization's leaders. Of course, goal setting in the public sector is also part of the process of policy formulation. In democratic theory, participation and deliberation are seen as forging and implementing policies that serve the common good (Elster, 1998; Habermas, 1995; Knight & Johnson, 1994). A general advantage of deliberation is that it aggregates disparate information (Surowiecki, 2004), but for those external to the organization, deliberation is also a way of establishing "buy-in." For those inside the organization, deliberation sets the stage for transforming organizational structures and standard operating procedures.

The third conceptual foundation is an emerging understanding of the essential role of *routines*, *rules*, and *procedures* in organizations (Becker, 2004; Nelson & Winter, 1982). Organizational routines, rules, and procedures – formal or informal – are the building blocks of organizations. They guide the day-to-day operation of agencies by connecting inputs to outputs and determine how agencies turn knowledge and resources into policy products. Routines organize knowledge in organizations, provide a language for communication, control discretion, and legitimize action (Feldman, 2000; March et al., 2000). Yet, routines, like all institutions, may be manipulated for reasons of efficiency or distribution – selecting "who gets what" (Knight, 1992; North, 1990). For organizational change to be real, deploying these goals brings about a broad variety of other changes in routines and rules; real change takes time as it permeates layers of hierarchy, working its way through layers of organizational routines (the "informal organization"). Change spreads as lower levels of organizational actors sequentially change the operating procedures they follow. Answering the question of whether change is efficient or distributive is only possible once all of the lower-level changes have been traced out.

These three themes help us better understand the core attributes of any change process. Leaders choose to set goals for organizations because goals are effective ways for inducing change; those goals can be set unilaterally or collectively through deliberation. The change process works its way through agencies by altering routines, rules, and procedures – a progression that requires many changes at successive layers of agency hierarchy. In many cases, these changes cause individual workers to perceive themselves as "worse off." These foundations help interpret the extended case presented in the following sections.

A Specific Structural Change: Matrix

At the CDC, debate centered on a basic structural choice. For decades, firms decided between functional (e.g., accounting, sales, or logistics) and product-line designs (e.g., brands). Product-line structures evolved because of communication overloads in functional structures (Williamson 1985, 281). Over time, scholars sought to merge them with alternative designs like the matrix organization to gain the benefits of both designs (Galbraith, 1974). Specifically, a matrix is supposed to take advantage of specialized expertise (technical or geographic) to become more innovative and flexible (Hatch, 2018, 41). They are used when the environment is complex and uncertain, there is pressure to share resources across product lines, and there is environmental pressure from critical inputs (Daft, 2007). Frequently, matrix form is used to let functional personnel work in cross-functional product teams, a more "organic" structure (Jones 2004, 183).

Importantly, for public organizations, authors use different terms for matrix organizations. Daft refers to "multifocused groupings" (having two structural grouping alternatives simultaneously), which may be called a matrix or a hybrid (Daft, 2007). The matrix dimensions can be product and geography groupings instead of "function and product" (Davis & Lawrence, 1978; Goggin, 1974; Jones, 2004). For example, a matrix public agency might have field employees report to both a local regional head and a functional boss, with the functional managers controlling annual performance appraisals of employees (Brickley, Smith, and Zimmerman 2004, 345). Yet, in practice, workers face dual supervision (a "two-boss" employee), which may make workers less responsive, more difficult to control, or less accountable (Bernheim & Whinston, 1986, 924; Jones, 2004, 183; Miller, 1992).

Empirically, matrix organizations show high levels of information processing and conflict referral (Ashkenas et al., 2002; Benedetto, 1985; Galbraith, 1974; Thompson, 2003).[1] Since the 1960s, numerous companies implemented matrix forms because of this flexibility, including ABB, Dow Corning, TRW, Kodak, Albany International, Club Med, Chrysler, and Xerox. Many were multileveled with cross-links between the organizational divisions, with two or more

---

[1] Matrix forms are different from "networks" and other adhocratic/organic organizational forms (Burns & Stalker, 1994, Mintzberg, 1979), (Mintzberg, 1979). Networks emphasize direct communication, negotiation, and shared decision-making (C. Jones et al., 1997).

hierarchies intersecting each other (Davis & Lawrence, 1977; Galbraith, 1974; Larson & Gobeli, 1988).

Matrix organizations increase the amount and types of conflict referred to higher levels of the hierarchy, refer conflict upward from the lowest organization levels, and reduce accountability of those who refer conflict upward. As such, common weaknesses include frustration and confusion from dual authority, enhanced training and interpersonal skills needs, costliness in time and need for conflict resolution, pressures on collegiality, and the need to maintain a balance of power (Daft, 2007, 111). Without stable expectations, employees often must negotiate over resource allocation (Davis & Lawrence, 1977; Larson & Gobeli, 1987). Consequently, recent appraisals show how hard it is to make matrix organizations work, calling them "all but unmanageable" (Fletcher and Taplin, 2002, 27).[2] Even if information technology (Meagher, 2003) or self-organizing workforces (Evans & Wolf, 2005) make it easier to overcome these challenges, efficiency may not be the most relevant consideration. Because matrix accelerates conflict and information referral, pressure increases for the executive but so does their relative power – and the same is true for boards and other overseers.

From firms, we know that organizations often "cycle" through different forms trying to find a way to keep information flowing and to refer conflict while also maintaining employee accountability throughout the organization. From function to product line, and from product line to matrix, and then back again – these changed day-to-day operations. As such, high-profile firms turned away from matrix in part because it is so difficult to implement in real organizations.

Agency Design in Political Settings

Public policy theorists widely recognize the important role of agenda setting in policy process models (Baumgartner & Jones, 1993; Birkland, 1997; Jones & Baumgartner, 2005; Majone, 2006). Likewise, we know that organizational charts winnow down or combine the choice sets available to decision-makers

---

[2] In the 1990s, Compaq abandoned matrix because of "tremendous pressure for change, especially from four levels down in the organization. Decisions weren't getting made because of the structure" (Ben Rosen quoted in Taylor, 1999, 126). The company was "decelerating, frankly, and organized in a matrix structure where no one had accountability" (Michael D. Capellas quoted in Lohr, 2002). Swiss corporation ABB was a well-known example of matrix: "the framework through which we organize our activities. It allows us to optimize our business globally and maximize performance in every country in which we operate. Some people resist it. They say the matrix is too rigid, too simplistic. But what choice do you have? To say you don't like a matrix is like saying you don't like factories or you don't like breathing. It's a fact of life." (Percy Barnevik quoted in Taylor, 1991, 95). By the 2000s, ABB had demonstrated that matrix forms are "difficult to manage", so it was abandoned (Ghemawat 2003, 80).

at different levels in the hierarchy: different organizational structures produce different agendas (or sequences of comparisons) for organizations. The organization's "agenda" depends on its internal communication channels (Arrow, 1974); organizational structure helps define the flow of information through the hierarchy (Hammond, 1986, 1994). By altering information flows and choice sequences in hierarchies, structures change organization-level outcomes (Hammond & Thomas, 1989).

We can think of organizational structure as playing the same role in hierarchies that institutions play in policy processes in how they aggregate preferences and information. Finding the policy that will satisfy most people depends on the rules of the game that are used for making political choices; the rules help determine where politics leads us. In this sense, agenda setters in politics try to use the rules to manipulate the outcome (perhaps even to benefit themselves).

This means that while finding "better" organizational structures is hard enough in firms (given the ways elements combine to produce firm-level outcomes), the game of organizational structuring is even harder in a world of public agencies. Choices about an agency's hierarchical structure help determine how public servants solve public problems by implementing public policies (Miller & Whitford, 2016; Moe, 1989; Wilson, 1989). As such, political overseers may manipulate the structure of government to open and close avenues of decision-making for individuals in organizations. In the "politics of bureaucratic structure," politicians seek to shape agencies through administrative reform (Lewis, 2003; Moe, 1989).

From a broad perspective, natural balancing of forces in politics means that rarely do politicians get what they desire; the agency's structure is a hybrid of competitive pushes. As a result, the structure is built for something entirely different from efficiency or effectiveness; it is an amalgamation of efficiency, effectiveness, distribution, fairness, and preferences over policy (both now and in the future). The agency is also a player in this game, but the agency is a "they" (not an "it"), with an internal political process populated by appointees and careerists (and heterogeneity in the views of both). Finally, civil servants may anticipate these dynamics and see the agency as prime for reshaping – that any structural outcome may be renegotiated; few institutional outcomes are set in stone.

Yet, even if politics permeates the process, actors debate design using a rhetoric founded in orthodox administrative theory (e.g., efficiency and effectiveness, control and economy). While we focus on traditional layers of reform (strategies, goals, and changes to routines, rules, and procedures) and specific structures like matrix, actors live in real public organizations and may see themselves as the targets of these broad political initiatives. There is a politics of agency design and reshaping that permeates the agency's life before, during, and after reorganization (Whitford, 2021).

Scientists and Reorganization

Understanding scientists living in policymaking organizations like the CDC thus leads to questions beyond the scope of most studies of agency reorganization. How do scientists react to the administrative ritual of reorganization? Are reform efforts in science-based organizations like the CDC different from the reorganization of the FBI or the DEA? How do processes like strategic change and goal setting interact with mechanisms of daily maintenance like routines and rules?

Questions like these drive the CDC reform narrative that follows, but they naturally lead to other, perhaps more difficult, questions about complex public organizations that depend on the work of scientists. For instance, should such agencies have new and different structures, unlike those dreamt up by organization theorists for firms like ABB? Should managers of government scientists develop new styles of leadership, or should they facilitate the emergence of new values and processes tailored to the habits and expectations of professional scientists? Should government scientists change their practices and beliefs to meld to the reform choices of the managerial generalists that usually lead their organizations?

Answering these broader questions is beyond the scope of the narrative offered here, but knowing something about this failed reform at CDC provides a measure of evidence about the work of government scientists and what happens when managers take on complex, deep, multiyear change processes in large government science organizations. We do not know what would have happened had this reform effort succeeded, but we can observe how reform as a ritual affected daily routines and how reform played out at both the macro level of the organization and the micro level of the workers who carried it out.

3 Strategic Change at the CDC

To better understand strategic change in public health science agencies like the CDC, it helps to see the variety of changes in the organization and configuration of national public health authorities during that time period: indeed, there is no universal selection among countries of the best organizational response to such matters. The US, the United Kingdom, Canada, and Australia have national authorities for the investigation of threats to public health and the delivery of programs intended to reduce those threats. But there is no one organizational model for these authorities; indeed, the goals stated for each agency – the local answer to "what is public health?" – themselves vary (Davis, 1998). But, over time, public health organizations emerged that are mostly actively engaged in the search for quality organizational responses to the public health threats of the next century. For this narrative, there is a common thread: public health agencies and their goals have changed over time. Before developing the CDC narrative, I briefly review important evolutionary changes in similar organizations.

The Broader Context

In 2003, the United Kingdom's Health Protection Agency (HPA) was created and charged with protecting the population from infectious diseases and other threats such as chemical hazards, poisons, and radiation. The HPA was an independent agency (a quasi-autonomous, nongovernmental organization [NGO] or "quango") that served the populations of England and Wales (Bertelli, 2006a, 2006b). It then merged with the National Radiological Protection Board in April 2005 to form a comprehensive health protection service and serve as a United Kingdom–wide body. Like other agencies of its type in other countries, the HPA was charged with responding to emerging threats related to bioterrorism and new disease strains. The HPA's core functions included identifying and responding to health hazards and emergencies, preparing for emerging threats, advising the public and Government on health protection, providing specialist health protection services, and supporting other agencies in health protection roles. The agency had over 2,700 employees for meeting its five-year *Corporate Plan* and strategic objectives (United Kingdom Health Protection Agency, 2004). To meet the plan's three core goals (and fourteen subgoals), the HPA was organized with three centers to implement fifteen programmes. It coordinated some activities with the UK's Environment Agency and coexisted with the Scottish Executive's new Health Protection Scotland to pursue the British government's national statement of public health and health policy objectives (first identified in the 1999 white paper *Saving Lives: Our Healthier Nation*; United Kingdom Department of Health and Social Care, 1999). In the constant dance of agency reorganization, the HPA was subsumed into Public Health England in 2013.

In contrast, the agency Health Canada remains responsible for helping maintain and improve public and individual health at the federal level. It develops policy, enforces regulations, promotes prevention for all Canadians, and delivers health services to indigenous communities. Its main role is maintaining the health insurance system. For threats to public health, Health Canada works through its Health Intelligence Network, branches, and component agencies, including the Public Health Agency of Canada (PHAC). Created in the wake of the Spanish flu of 1918, Health Canada named its first-ever chief public health officer in September 2004 to oversee a ten-year action plan intended to focus on efforts to prevent chronic diseases, prevent injuries, and respond to public health emergencies and threats from infectious disease (Public Health Agency of Canada, 2005a). The PHAC was created to foster expanded coordination and collaboration among governments, academia, researchers, and NGOs by configuring six National Collaborating Centres for Public Health: Determinants of Health; Public Policy and Risk Assessment; Infrastructure, Info-Structure and New Tools Development; Infectious Diseases; Environmental Health; and Aboriginal Health. Canadian statements about overall public health and health policy objectives for the country included the *Integrated Pan-Canadian Healthy Living Strategy* (Public Health Agency of Canada, 2005b).

In Australia, the Department of Health and Ageing's Population Health Division (PHD) was charged with overseeing the national response on communicable diseases, immunization, nutrition and obesity, physical activity, food policy, smoking, and substance abuse. As part of a federal-state-private sector partnership, PHD delivered childhood immunizations; worked to ensure the safety of air, food, and water supplies; and monitored and responded to infectious disease threats. It is notable that the Department of Health and Ageing was active on these issues (in various guises) since 1921, partly due to the early history of the population health/sanitarian movement in Australia. Its 2003–2005 *Corporate Plan* offered six comprehensive (although vague) goals for the Department and its divisions: to promote equitable access, to foster a healthier community, to broaden primary care with better links to community and acute care, to ensure choice and access for aged care services, to improve choice from a mixture of public and private health sectors, and to work toward a sustainable health system that responds to new pressures while limiting cost (Australia Department of Health and Ageing, 2003). The Department and PHD worked with several other agencies, including the Australian Institute of Health and Welfare, the Australian Radiation Protection and Nuclear Safety Agency, and Food Standards Australia New Zealand, to release statements of national health objectives. The Department was dissolved in 2013 to become part of the Australian Department of Health.

Most notably, in May 2005, the European Centre for Disease Prevention and Control (ECDC) was launched as a way of expanding cooperation among member states of the European Union (EU), the European Commission, the World Health Organization, and other countries. It replaced the Commission's Communicable Diseases Network, in operation since 1999, which was an ad hoc mechanism for cooperation.[3] This new EU agency was charged with providing an integrated approach to controlling communicable diseases and other health threats, as well as expanding synergies among existing national centers for disease control.

Main tasks have included: epidemiological surveillance and networking of laboratories at the European level, early warning and response, scientific opinions based on independent scientific evidence through EU-wide networks and ad hoc scientific panels, and technical assistance and communication in European countries and (if necessary) countries outside the EU (European Centre for Disease Prevention and Control, 2005). To meet these challenges, the ECDC organized around four units (scientific advice, surveillance and communication, preparedness and response, and management and administration). Its guiding EU statements on public health and health policy objectives have included the 2007 *Together for Health* (Commission of the European Communities, 2007).

The central thread here is that public health science agencies around the world must often change in response to new directives.

New Directives for the CDC

My focus here, though, is on how the US CDC deliberated over the future of public health, made decisions about what its core goals were for public health and how they should be attained, and how it sought to deploy those policies and programs throughout the agency. Specifically, the CDC's leaders, staff, and partners sought to answer the question "what is public health?" through strategic visioning in the Futures Initiative, the CDC's first reorganization in the twenty-five years since its creation in 1946 (Etheridge, 1992).

The experiences of the CDC, along with those of other countries struggling to redefine public health in a world of emerging threats, are bound together in three important ways. First, these attempts to reenvision public health have common purposes, processes, and timing regarding responses to key public health challenges. Second, it is clear from the CDC's experiences that reenvisioning public health had substantial external consequences beyond immediate organizational reform, for leaders in government, customers, and members of the public health community. Third, reenvisioning has had clear impacts on agency structures, operations, human capital, and leadership.

As noted previously, in the US, as commentators have weighed in on public health's identity and contours, reports like the 1988 IOM report *The Future of*

---

[3] See Decision 2119/98/EC. Available at: https://eur-lex.europa.eu/legal-content/EN/ALL/?uri=CELEX%3A31998D2119.

Public Health focused on the interaction between the level of scientific and technical knowledge but also called for greater involvement by the public in determining priority health goals and services. The responses that followed came even as the CDC was regarded as an agency with a clear purpose and strong performance. A January 2007 Harris Poll showed that 90 percent of respondents indicated that they knew what the CDC does (up from 85 percent in 2001) and that 84 percent of those respondents said the agency did an excellent or pretty good job (up from 79 percent in 2001). The CDC faced growing concern about its capacity for handling new and emerging threats to public health, yet average Americans saw the CDC as doing a good job.

In the US, the Department of Health and Human Services (HHS) is charged with protecting the health of Americans and providing human services. The core US Public Health Service (PHS) agencies include the CDC and other agencies like the National Institutes of Health (NIH), the Food and Drug Administration (FDA), and the Health Resources and Services Administration; HHS also includes other PHS agencies and other prominent units such as the Centers for Medicare & Medicaid Services.

The CDC is often regarded as the frontline HHS agency for public health. It works with the states and other partners to provide health surveillance, monitors emerging disease threats (including bioterrorism), formulates and implements strategies for the prevention of disease (including chronic diseases), maintains data on health statistics, regulates the provision of immunization services, regulates workplace safety, makes policy for the prevention of environmental disease, and investigates and safeguards against international disease transmission. The CDC was established in 1946 as the Communicable Disease Center; in the 1980s, it was renamed the Centers for Disease Control, and the word "Prevention" was added in 1992. A relatively recent innovation in the fight to maintain public health (Duffy, 1990), the CDC's mission has grown from fighting malaria and other communicable diseases to promoting "health and quality of life by preventing and controlling disease, injury, and disability."

Historically, the CDC holds three "core values": (1) accountability that research and services are rooted in sound science and targeted at real public health needs and goals; (2) respect, an understanding of the contributions and value of individual and cultural diversity, both inside and outside the agency; and (3) honesty, ethical activity, and scientific integrity (Centers for Disease Control and Prevention, 2004a). The CDC pursues these values by the actions of employees working across 170 job occupations. During the time period under discussion here, the CDC's workforce was 78 percent civil service staff, 10 percent PHS Commissioned Corps, and 12 percent contractors (U.S. Government

Accountability Office 2004, 7). In fiscal year (FY) 2007, the CDC budget was $5.8 billion, and it had 9,000 full-time equivalents.

In 2003, Dr. Julie Gerberding, Director of the CDC for then just a year, began the Futures Initiative to define key health protection goals for focusing national and organizational attention and to completely reform the agency's goals and organization (see Table 1). The Futures Initiative set out to strategically plan the CDC's future and act as a catalyst for changing public health policy and organization (Centers for Disease Control and Prevention, 2003) and was in a quiet phase for a year before being formally announced to the public in May 2004. This process was systematic and comprehensive – ranging from the overhaul of business and human capital management systems to the design and deployment of readiness teams and systems for future public health emergencies.

First, the Futures Initiative used a broadly deliberative process for selecting objectives. The CDC staff collected input and comments from a broad selection of CDC employees, "partners," and "customers" – in total, more than 500 individuals and organizations participated in the process of deliberating over and selecting objectives. Participation took place through a dazzling array of means, including the first agency-wide employee surveys (with a robust 53 percent response rate; Neslund et al., 2004), one-on-one interviews, discussion groups, emails, meetings of stakeholders, and satellite teleconferences using the CDC's national Public Health Training Network (a distance learning platform). By including current and potential "customers," the CDC built contacts with people whose health is the target of the agency's actions. "Partners" included national, state, and local public health organizations, public health workers, and clinicians. This group also included professional and medical associations, community-based organizations, foundations, and business and private sector entities. The process also sought the input of priority populations and advocates.

Specifically, the Futures Initiative involved customers, partners, channels, and other stakeholders through a series of discussion groups over a period of

Table 1 Core components of strategic transformation at the CDC

Core Component 1: The Futures Initiative used a broadly deliberative process for selecting objectives.

Core Component 2: Based on this deliberative process, the Futures Initiative developed six strategic directions for the CDC and its programs and adopted two overarching health protection goals.

Core Component 3: These goals guided a complete restructuring of the CDC's organizational structure, personnel systems, and planned expenditures.

months intended to uncover key concerns they might have about the CDC, as well as identify areas of strength. The CDC employees and managers recognized that building a deliberative process for setting goals had both benefits and costs. One early planning document showed how people weighed what should be the breadth and depth of public participation – that options involved both pros and cons (Centers for Disease Control and Prevention, Agency for Toxic Substances and Disease Registry, 2004).

This self-described "outside-in" review provided numerous opportunities for partners, customers, and employees to engage one another, given the difficulty of assessing increasingly complex, value-laden, and often competing priorities. In public health circles, deliberative public involvement (a cornerstone of the Futures Initiative) has been seen as promoting discussion and delivering more informed and consensual views (Abelson, Eyles, et al., 2003; Abelson, Forest, et al., 2003).[4] This is seen in the deliberation model as "consult, involve, and collaborate" (see Figure 1), a model familiar to people working in activities like health promotion and marketing. While it was recognized that "involve" and "collaborate" ceded some control over final outcomes to partners, the CDC devoted significant resources to listening to partners and involving them in the planning process.

Second, based on this deliberative process, the Futures Initiative developed six strategic directions for the CDC and its programs: (1) the CDC should prioritize its science, research, and programs in order to achieve

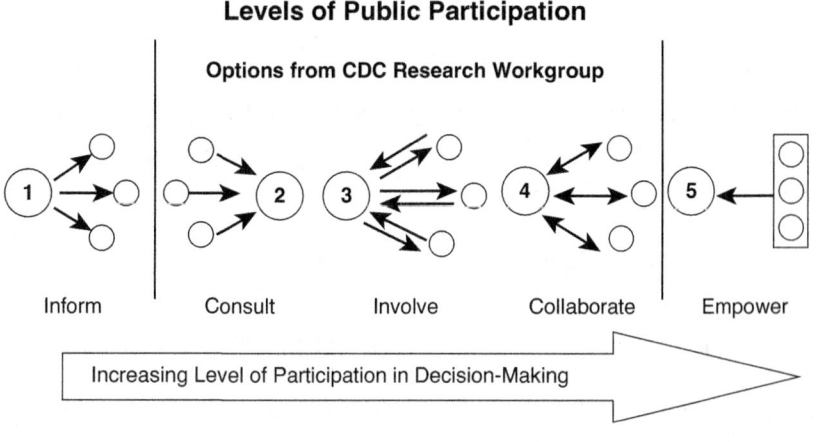

Figure 1 Deliberation model

---

[4] This approach (and CDC implemented it) is now referred to as a "small world" network approach for health protection (McDowell, 2005). "Small world" networks are a way of connecting multiple seemingly disconnected stakeholders (Travers & Milgram, 1977).

measurable health impact for the public and emphasize prevention of early risk factors and support of healthy behaviors; (2) the CDC should have their customers (those whose health the CDC is working to protect) as the central focus of the organization; (3) CDC programs, policies, and practices should be based on scientific research; (4) the CDC should assume greater leadership in strengthening the health impact of state and local public health systems; (5) the CDC should have clear priorities for global programs and become better able to provide rapid detection and response to emerging health threats; and (6) the CDC should become more efficient, effective, and accountable by modernizing its management and business practices.

Given these strategic directions, the Futures Initiative argued that the deployment of organizational resources should be in accord with two overarching health protection goals: (1) health promotion and prevention: all people will achieve their optimal lifespan with the best possible quality of health in every stage of life. This includes those at higher risk due to health disparities; and (2) preparedness: communities will be protected from infectious, occupational, environmental, and terrorist threats (see Table 2).

Establishing national and organizational goals for public health is almost a cottage industry for HHS. *Healthy People*, the 1979 Surgeon General's

Table 2 Six strategic directions and two overarching goals

Strategic Direction 1: The CDC should prioritize its science, research, and programs in order to achieve measurable health impact for the public and emphasize prevention of early risk factors and support of healthy behaviors.

Strategic Direction 2: The CDC should have their customers (those whose health the CDC is working to protect) as the central focus of the organization.

Strategic Direction 3: The CDC programs, policies, and practices should be based on scientific research.

Strategic Direction 4: The CDC should assume greater leadership in strengthening the health impact of state and local public health systems.

Strategic Direction 5: The CDC should have clear priorities for global programs and become better able to provide rapid detection and response to emerging health threats.

Strategic Direction 6: The CDC should become more efficient, effective, and accountable by modernizing its management and business practices.

Goal 1: Health promotion and prevention: all people will achieve their optimal lifespan with the best possible quality of health in every stage of life.

Goal 2: Preparedness: communities will be protected from infectious, occupational, environmental, and terrorist threats.

Report, laid the groundwork for a national prevention agenda (Public Health Service, Office of the Assistant Secretary for Health and Surgeon General, U.S. Department of Health, Education, and Welfare, 1979). *Promoting Health/ Preventing Disease: Objectives for the Nation* (Public Health Service, U.S. Department of Health and Human Services, 1980) and *Healthy People 2000: National Health Promotion and Disease Prevention Objectives* (Public Health Service, U.S. Department of Health and Human Services, 1991) followed; both sought to establish national health objectives and spur the development of state and community plans. The Office of Disease Prevention and Health Promotion's *Healthy People 2010* (U.S. Department of Health and Human Services, 2011) also had two goals: to increase the quality and years of healthy life and to eliminate health disparities among different segments of the population. Healthy People 2020 followed.

These goals have consequences. They are used for assessing progress made under numerous programs (e.g., the Indian Health Care Improvement Act, the Maternal and Child Health Block Grant, the Preventive Health and Health Services Block Grant). They are used in performance measurement activities (e.g., the Health Plan Employer Data and Information Set). Indeed, *Healthy People 2010*'s vision – healthy people in healthy communities – was made the starting point for the IOM's *The Future of the Public's Health in the 21st Century*. However, the goals set out in Healthy People 2010 were not specific enough for the CDC when developing strategies in the Futures Initiative (e.g., for performance measurement and benchmarking).

Third, these deliberations guided a complete restructuring of the CDC's organizational structure, personnel systems, and planned expenditures. Staff members and advisors used the input for determining the CDC's new organizational design. The CDC had been divided into twelve national centers, institutes, and offices composed of divisions, branches, and sections. The reorganization brought four new Coordinating Centers, two coordinating offices, and two new centers to augment the previous structure. The four Coordinating Centers were: (1) the Coordinating Center for Infectious Disease, which houses the National Center for Infectious Diseases (NCID), the National Immunization Program, and the National Center for HIV/AIDS, Viral Hepatitis, STD, and TB Prevention; (2) the Coordinating Center for Environmental and Occupational Health and Injury Prevention (including the Agency for Toxic Substances and Disease Registry [ATSDR] and national centers for Environmental Health and Injury Prevention and Control); (3) the Coordinating Center for Health Promotion (including the Office of Genomics and Disease Prevention and national centers for Birth Defects and Developmental Disabilities and Chronic Disease Prevention and Health

Promotion); and (4) the Coordinating Center for Public Health and Information Services (including the National Center for Health Statistics, the National Center for Health Marketing, and the National Center for Public Health Informatics). The coordinating offices were Terrorism Preparedness and Emergency Response and Global Health. The two new centers were Public Health Informatics and Health Marketing. The National Institute for Occupational Safety and Health (NIOSH) remained separate and intact from the previous structure.

Under the old design, the CDC Director had to oversee vastly disparate programs. The reorganization added management capacity, including offices of Career and Workforce Development, a Chief Science Officer, Enterprise Communication, Public Health Practice, and Strategy and Innovation. More importantly, the "old CDC" relied heavily on hierarchy, but the "new CDC" had a matrix structure (a "heterarchical" form) to improve organizational flexibility and information sharing. The CDC's primary challenges are almost always nonroutine, and matrix forms were thought to work well in nonroutine task environments. Heterarchies are matrix organizations – multileveled with cross-links between divisions because two or more hierarchies intersect with one another (Davis & Lawrence, 1977). As noted previously, the theory was that the matrix would reduce information overloads and improve information aggregation. In this case, the new structure was a modified internal network (Mintzberg, 1979). It depended on direct communication and negotiation among units (read Coordinating Centers) and emphasized shared decision-making (Jones et al., 1997).

Before elaborating more on this specific choice, it is worthwhile reiterating how this process fits with the strategic choice model presented in Section 2. Generally, this change process, led by strategic action on the part of the CDC's leadership, used deliberation for deciding new organizational goals; based on those goals, it charted a course leading to change in routines, rules, and procedures throughout the organization. As in other cases worldwide, goal setting at the CDC was intended to reenvision the contours of public health.

Just as the choice to take strategic action was crucial, so was the choice of Gerberding to be Director as her beliefs and incentives were reflected in efforts to transform the CDC. Gerberding brought important "framing" experiences with her that shaped her focus on issues of direction and control. Namely, as Acting Deputy Director of the NCID, she played a major (if not the key) role in managing the CDC's response to the 2001 anthrax events, as one of the main "faces" of the public relations effort (Kettl, 2005). As the CDC describes this triggering event, "In 2001, powdered anthrax spores were deliberately put into letters that were mailed through the U.S. postal system. Twenty-two people, including 12 mail handlers, got anthrax, and five of these 22 people died" (Centers for Disease Control and Prevention, 2014).

In this case, the form and purpose of deliberation were also key because how views are aggregated helps determine what people think agencies should be doing and why (Knight & Johnson, 1994) and how that view should be represented in the agency's routines, rules, and processes. Over twenty-two months, staff, partners, and customers of the CDC deliberated over a common view of the contours of public health, one that went beyond other HHS-based goals statements because everyone knew its strategic purpose was to transform the CDC. Yet, unlike other countries, the CDC did not simply adopt the national goals (*Healthy People 2010*) as its goals. The Futures Initiative decided goals for the express purpose of reorganizing the CDC.

Is the CDC's future important? Of course, the goals policymakers set for improving American public health are often ignored; similarly, the CDC's focus shifts as new problems arise and old ones fade away – malaria is now a low priority in the US, but coronavirus and Zika have emerged. Even so, setting goals is fundamental for leaders searching to improve performance, and strategic visioning is widely considered useful for setting goals and "fixing" large, complex organizations. But never had the CDC, as the peak American public health organization, invested so much in "from the ground up" (or in CDC terms, "outside-in") deliberation about the contours of American public health. This combination of deliberation, decision, and deployment made the CDC an important lens on the future of public health science organizations.

The next section focuses on the reform of the CDC's structure from a traditional hierarchy, long marked by organizational "silos," to a new matrix (or N-form, heterarchical) structure to enhance organizational flexibility and information sharing. In advocating for a matrix form, the Futures Initiative embedded some known flaws. These flaws help us understand the distress experienced by the CDC's science professionals, leading to the reorganization's ultimate demise.

From Silos to Matrix at the CDC

Before the Futures Initiative, the Director was supported by twelve administrative support units in the Office of the Director (OD) but was also responsible for a broad array of "direct reports" (Figure 2). The CDC's core eleven national centers were the way the CDC worked with external partners, its "customers" or target populations, and channels (including governmental and nongovernmental connections between the CDC and its customers). Each center was an important source of assistance (e.g., training, funding) for the CDC's partners; in FY 2002,

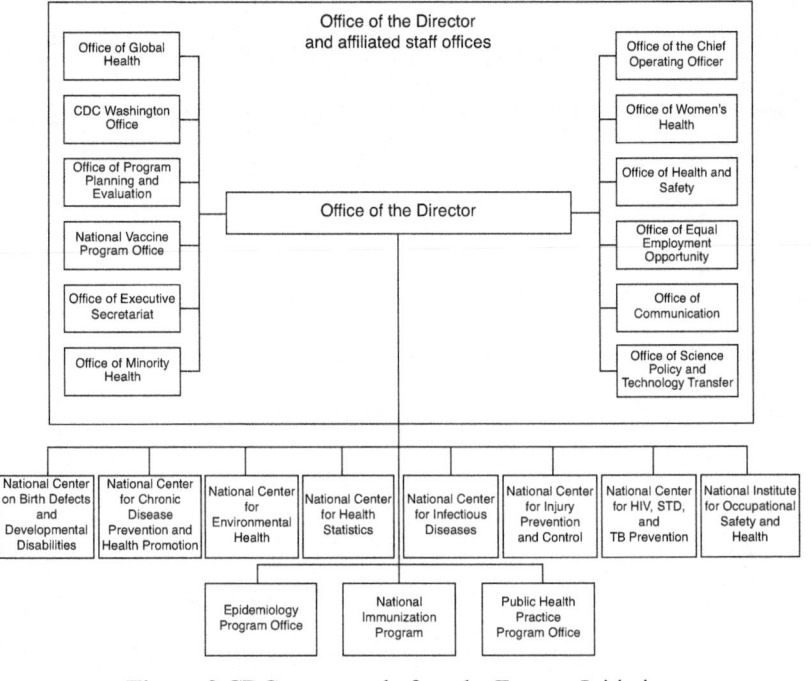

Figure 2 CDC structure before the Futures Initiative
Source: CDC and Government Accountability Office (GAO; 2004)

69 percent of the CDC's budget went to partners through cooperative agreements and grants (75 percent to state health departments; U.S. Government Accountability Office 2004, 7). Each was a mini agency with a director's office, divisions and branches, and budget. Many had their own mission statements and several their own strategic plans (U.S. Government Accountability Office 2004, 10). The Director also served as Administrator of the ATSDR, historically a separate PHS agency. ATSDR and the National Center for Environmental Health combined administrative and management functions in 2003.

The Director and OD staffers were responsible for directing this diverse set of centers and for coordinating all of the scientific and medical programs in those centers (Figure 3). That arrangement was only adopted in 2003 in response to perceived failures in control and performance. The CDC lacked financial controls over the centers (U.S. Department of Health and Human Services, Office of Inspector General, 1999; U.S. Government Accountability Office, 2000b). The agency was criticized for slow response times in the cases of West Nile virus and anthrax (U.S. Government Accountability Office, 2000a) and over the control of biological agents (U.S. Government Accountability Office, 2002). The 2004 GAO study followed up on these reports to see how the CDC was responding to perceptions of a lack of financial and other controls.

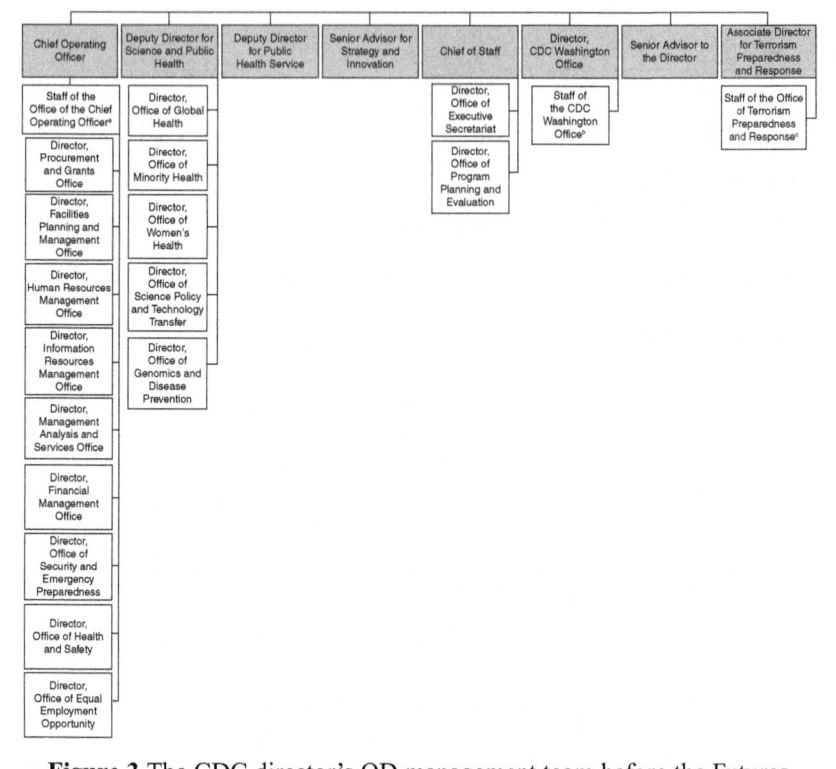

Figure 3 The CDC director's OD management team before the Futures
Initiative

Source: CDC and GAO (2004)

One response was the creation of Chief Operating Officer (COO), with oversight responsibility for financial management, control and reporting technologies,
and control of operations units. Other innovations included the strengthening of
the Office of Communications (Figure 4). Yet, before the Futures Initiative, the
Director herself had primary responsibility for line control over the CDC centers;
OD was weak; and the COO had little information for actual control.

The creation of COO, though, had a significant impact because, in 2003,
Director Gerberding named William (Bill) H. Gimson to the position. Having
been head of the Financial Management Office since 1996, Gimson had significant
field experience (fourteen years as a public health advisor) and had completed
managerial rotations. More importantly, he had an MBA from the Fuqua School of
Business at Duke University – an unusual pedigree for a manager in a traditional
public health organization like the CDC. In a 2006 Financial Times article about
Duke's Global Executive MBA training program, Gimson said, "We want to make
the CDC an exemplar of good governance, marrying the best of the private sector

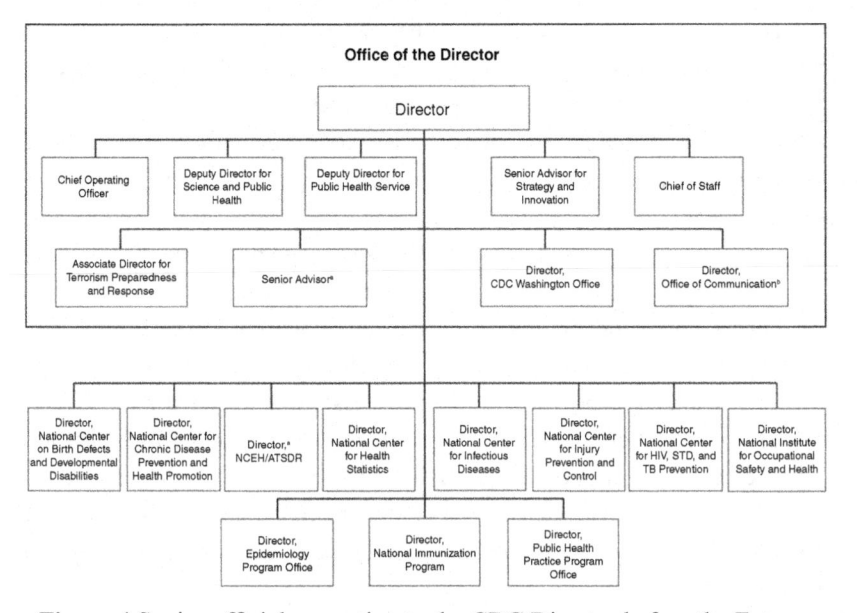

Figure 4 Senior officials reporting to the CDC Director before the Futures Initiative

Source: CDC and GAO (2004)

with the best of the public sector" (Ward, 2006). Gimson became a central figure in the Futures Initiative. However, he was not the only business influence as Gerberding also sought advice on this reorganization from Kent Nelson, a local Atlanta businessman on the CDC Foundation board who reorganized United Parcel Service as its chief executive officer (Young, 2006f).

The 2004 GAO report commended the CDC for improvement of the OD's ability to oversee public health emergency responses by moving from running four separate emergency operation centers to a central command-and-control center. The GAO report also found many remaining problems: the CDC could not easily monitor the centers' programmatic activities, lacked formal communication channels between OD staff and the centers; could not track center activities and schedules; could not influence center agendas; and could not force collaboration (U.S. Government Accountability Office, 2004, 4). It also faced looming human capital challenges from retirements – a challenge not unique to the CDC but one that substantially affected the reorganization process.

While the CDC's outside-in strategy of public deliberation produced goals, implementation was left to the CDC's senior leadership. Seeing needs to enhance collaboration, reduce silos within the organization, and reduce the number of direct reports to the Director, the work group chose a structure with Coordinating Centers as collection points for groups of centers. The

May 2004 final design reduced the number of direct reports from twenty-three to thirteen and created the six Coordinating Centers/offices (see Figure 5; Centers for Disease Control and Prevention, 2004b).

The resulting structures operated by "matrixing" key individuals within the Coordinating Centers/offices so that they were simultaneously members of both the centers/offices and the management offices now located in OD; this included chief management officials (CMOs), strategy and innovation officers, enterprise communication officers, science officers, public health practice officers, and other people such as writers/editors. For instance, the Office of Strategy and Innovation sent officers to other centers. As managers working in offices largely composed of science professionals, they were to "institutionalize organizational change, improvement and accountability," "participate in discussions of overall goals and strategies at the coordinating center level," and refine "goals, measures, and identification and creation of new or enhanced high priority programmatic areas" (Centers for Disease Control and Prevention, 2005).

The managers saw matrix as the clear way forward. The CDC Networking and Matrix Management Team recommended matrix management in 2005.

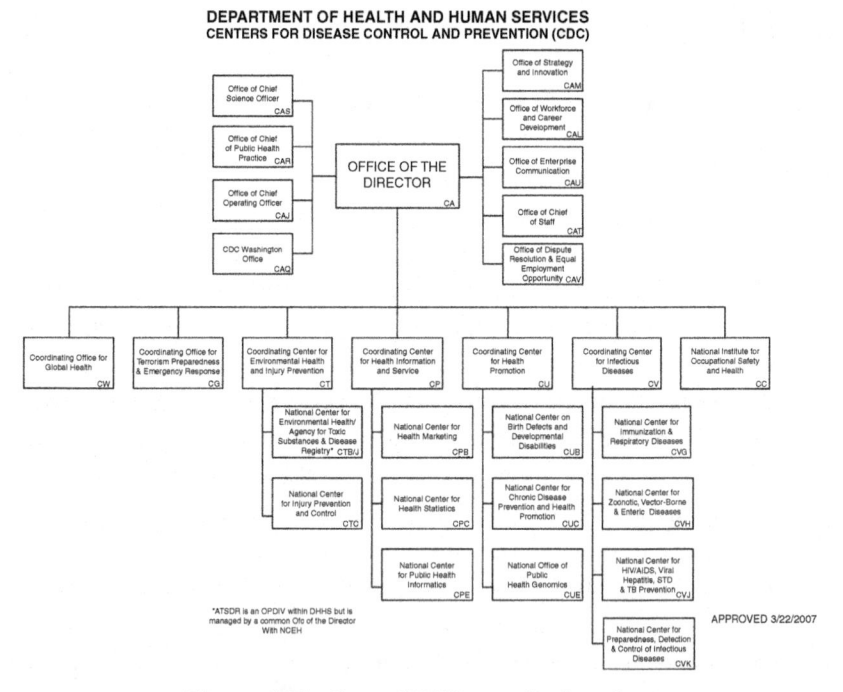

Figure 5 The "new CDC" organization chart

Source: CDC

HHS Secretary Michael O. Leavitt argued that matrix was "the next frontier of human productivity. We've had the agricultural age, the industrial age, the information age. The next era is the era of interoperability" (quoted in Carver, 2005). This may not be surprising: the GAO study called for the use of cross-functional or "matrixed" team organizational designs (U.S. Government Accountability Office, 2004, 23). Indeed, one former CDC director said that the CDC's reorganization as a set of "Centers" in the 1970s placed a premium on "matrix management" in the case of disease outbreaks (Foege, 2006).

A primary difficulty is defining exactly what is a matrix and what it means for those who operate in such a structure. Matrix changed the Director's direct reports, but it also changed the type and range of reports for everyone else in the system as it changed the flow of information and conflict within the organization (Whitford, 2006). Figure 6 shows three prototypes that were considered; using these, the Ad Hoc Committee on health promotion functions struggled to find a way to show what all this would mean for workers deciding the "who, what, why, and when" of their everyday operations with others (Centers for Disease Control and Prevention, Health Promotion and Education, 2004). In a less-than-clear directive, the report says that Gerberding announced in an all-staff memo that the agency "would be pursuing a variation of Prototype A, with enhancements from Prototype B. Prototype A, which retains the best features of our current structure, relies on centers that integrate science and program. Prototype

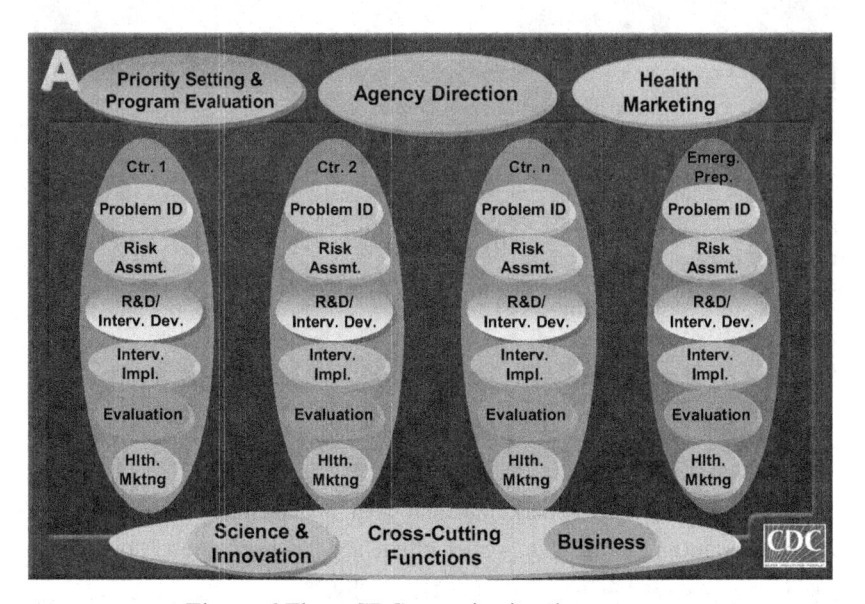

Figure 6 Three CDC organizational prototypes
Source: CDC

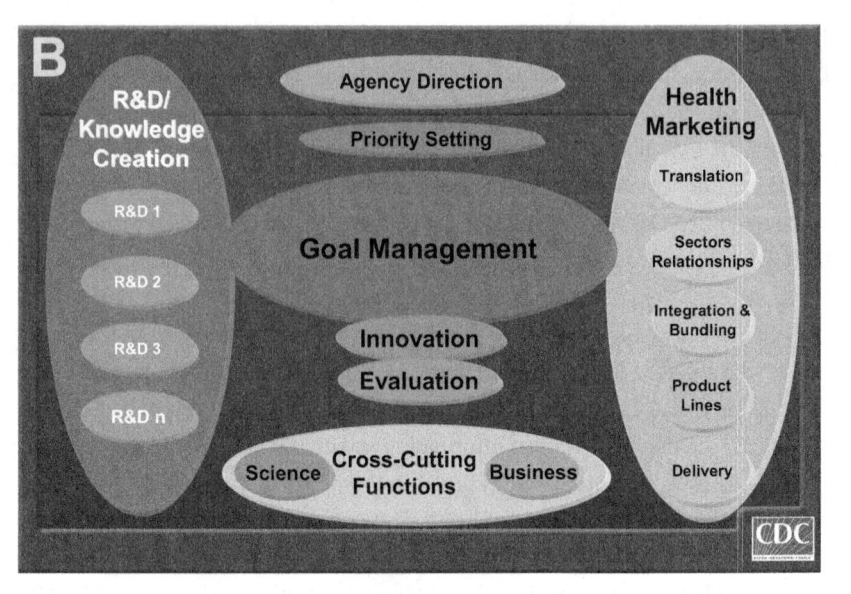

Figure 6 Cont.

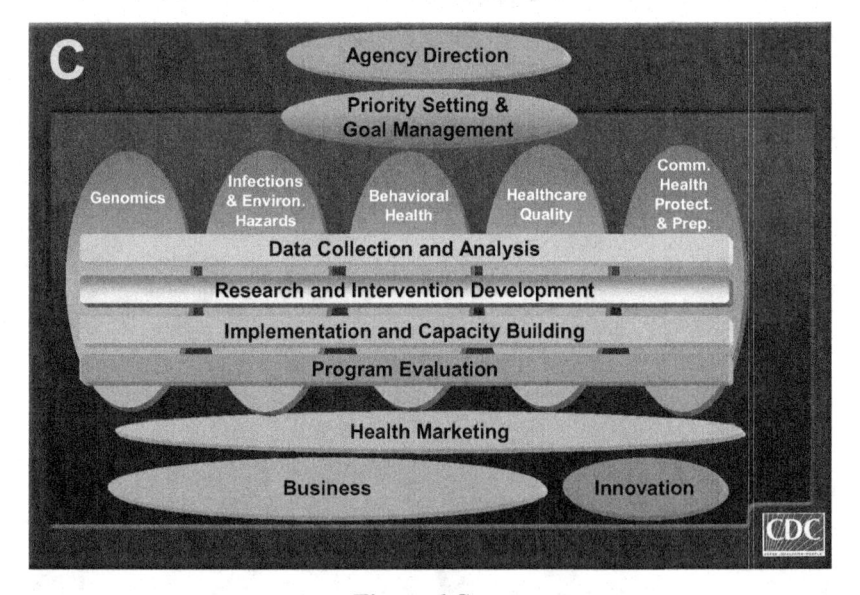

Figure 6 Cont.

B includes robust health marketing and goal management functions." The choice was meant to "achieve greater efficiency and integration," to enhance the "crosscutting functions of CDC program offices."

This signals how often practitioners struggle to fit together organizational design concepts and the practical aspects of their jobs, using language like this:

"In Prototype A, a health promotion focal point would be consistent with the 'Customer Interface' component in the sub-area entitled 'Systems Integration.' In Prototype B support for a health promotion focal point is integral to the specific 'Cross Cutting Functions' component" (Centers for Disease Control and Prevention, Health Promotion and Education, 2004). Interestingly, in the end, the most complex prototypes were set aside because agency veterans warned that they endangered the CDC's relationships with partners like the state health departments and laboratories (McKenna, 2004).

At a practical level, each unit inside one of the CDC's traditional centers of activity needed to know how they related to the rest of the organization and how the rest of the organization related to them. For instance, the Coordinating Center for Health Information and Science saw their role within the CDC as a bridge between the organization and the broad array of "people whose health we can improve," including partners, alliances, channels, and stakeholders (see Figure 7). As just one of the six centers/offices, the coordinating center served

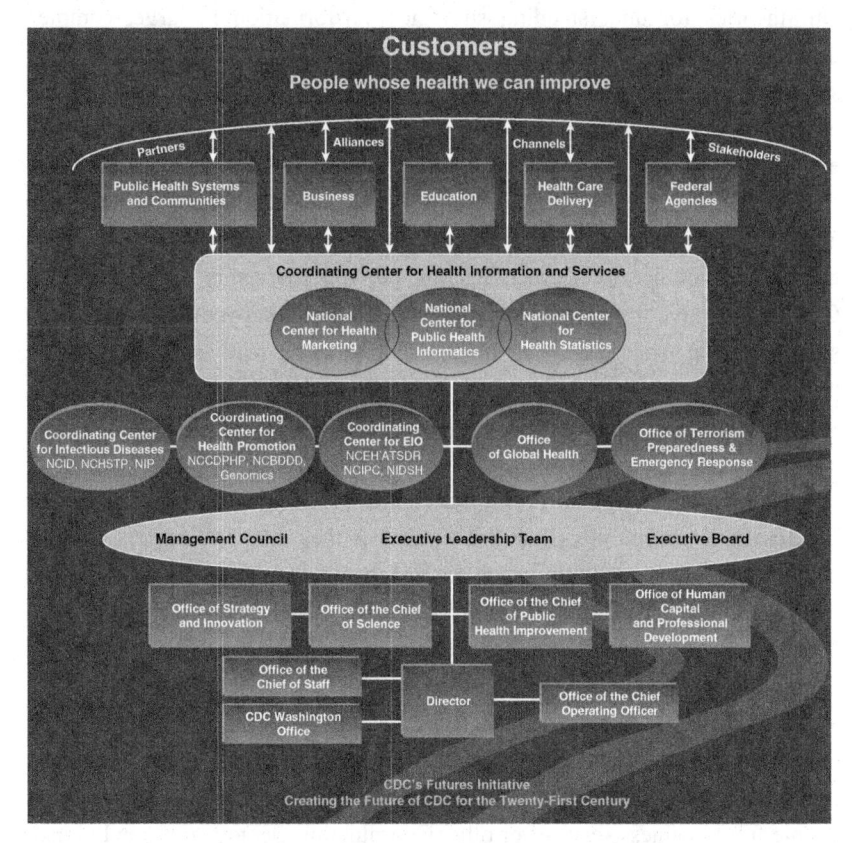

Figure 7 Proposed organization chart

Source: CDC

as a nexus between the agency and outside groups – but they were not the only ones. The Futures Initiative made it clear that other units stood between them and the Director.

These are the changes matrix management was supposed to bring to the CDC. After reorganization, the Director would rely on a system of networked governance through three top-level leadership groups for establishing and monitoring the agency's overall direction, supplemented by matrixed individuals throughout the CDC. The Executive Leadership Team would be responsible for strategic decisions about policy and investments regarding science, programs, and operations. The Management Council would govern management practices in support of the strategy. The directors of the twelve centers, institutes, and offices would be jointly responsible for overseeing the quality and integrity of the CDC's science and public health programs.

Discussion

Our theories for understanding strategic transformation in large, complex organizations suggest that leaders take strategic action, that they find ways to set credible goals for their employees, and that they then worry about how to change the routines, rules, and procedures that operate in the everyday work environment. Hierarchical change at the CDC was a result of all these elements.

First, hierarchical change – the shift from a more traditional product-line approach to organizing the work world of employees at the CDC – is rooted in the strategic choice by Gerberding and her top leadership team (including Gimson) to move the agency forward even though it enjoyed historically high support among Americans. This move occurred along with an extended GAO probe of the agency that began in June 2002, just as Gerberding became Director, and continued until January 2004, after the CDC had begun the deliberations seen as necessary for gaining agreement by their partners for large-scale change.

Second, goal setting is a potent mechanism for reorganization. Early in the Futures Initiative, partners made it clear that they saw the centers as silos hindering policies that could match the task environment partners saw in local areas. Certain critical events – like anthrax and the advent of the West Nile virus – helped focus attention on silos. One central goal that came out of that process was the need for greater collaboration among the CDC's centers and offices.

Third, in the end, the problem for leaders was to change how 9,000 people do their work daily – work that is governed by packages of routines, rules, and procedures. In the CDC's acceptance of matrix, the focus was on detailing people from business services or other Coordinating Centers to the individual, science-oriented centers to change how those organizations worked. At the same time, reorganization called for the same kind of "networking" at higher levels with councils that joined together business operations people and those with specific scientific and/or public health interests.

The language of organizational change within the CDC reflected the need to make matrix management work in a large, complex organization. In interviews, senior staff regularly referred to "goal-action plans" and "solution managers," with a premium put on horizontal communication. The overall approach leaned heavily on organizational transformation processes advocated by John P. Kotter, Harvard Business School professor and leading authority on private sector leadership and change (Kotter, 2012). The strategy was described as coming from the "Kotter playbook."

Yet, theory and experience from the business world suggest that in several important cases, firms have moved away from matrix designs because they are so hard in practice to implement – that in practice, it takes a special set of leaders to build the kinds of routines, rules, and procedures that must be in place to supplement the matrix. Matrix asks individuals inside the matrix to react to its indeterminacy and the natural inclination to move conflict upward in the hierarchy by creating supplementary institutions (rules) that select when the matrix should operate and how they should make up for it.

The next section returns to the central theme of this Element: that the herding of science professionals through managerial tools like reorganization is a tricky enterprise. Part of this is a story about the leadership of the CDC's Futures Initiative, but the variety of problems shows that managerialism and science professionals are always in an uneasy truce. As such, reorganization faces the following challenge: How to harness the power of scientists in the creation and implementation of public policy without compromising the reasons they chose the job in the first place.

4 Reactions to Reform Efforts

Organization theorists have long recognized that organizational leaders are important if only when they can help others make sense of complex environments and action landscapes (Weick, 1995). In change environments like those where leaders try to strategically transform large, complex organizations, individuals vary in how they interpret events as the change process unfolds (Isabella, 1990). There are four stages in how individuals interpret such events (anticipation, confirmation, culmination, and aftermath), so "resistances to change might alternatively be viewed, not as obstacles to overcome, but as inherent elements of the cognitive transition occurring during change" (Isabella, 1990, 34). What matters then is understanding how frames of reference such as mistrust, self-interest, or preference for the status quo shape how employees come to terms with change.

Yet, some reactions are likely – even understandable – during far-reaching strategic transformation. Moreover, how line and staff react to critical events in the context of organizational change helps us understand what cognitive responses follow which actions in public sector reorganization. In some organizations, specific reactions are almost guaranteed because of how science professionals make sense of the organizational world they inhabit.

In this section, I offer three ways of examining those reactions. The first centers on the response to one specific proposed structural change. The second centers on responses to a series of small events. The third turns to the reactions of the workers and how outside actors perceived those reactions. These elements help address how workers see the reorganization process and how events shape their perceptions of the culmination and aftermath of organizational change. In the following section, I offer a data-based picture of changes in morale from this reorganization as measured by a widely used federal employee attitudes data set.

Broadly speaking, though, the Futures Initiative was more than a compilation of events surrounding strategic choices by top leadership at the CDC – it was a continuum of activities that included local public health officials watching the announcements on the CDC's Public Health Training Network, Gerberding testifying to Congress about the proposed reorganization, and even anonymous blogs by careerists of their responses to the Futures Initiative on the now-dormant site "www.cdcchatter.net." Together these moving parts and individuals – both inside and outside the CDC – helped determine reorganization's outcomes.

The Revolt of External and Professional Associations

After the May 2004 announcement of intent to reorganize, opposition soon formed to the proposal that the NIOSH director would report to the head of the new Coordinating Center for Environmental Health, Injury Prevention, and Occupational Health rather than directly to the Director. According to a former NIOSH official, the problem was not that "the primary purpose of CDC reorganization was to inhibit NIOSH from performing its mission, but . . . that will be the effect" (quoted in Inside OSHA, 2004a). Historically, NIOSH retained connections with the Occupational Safety and Health Administration (OSHA; they were created at the same time in 1970), with NIOSH handling scientific investigations while OSHA promulgated rules. The concern was that the coordinating center matrix framework would replace NIOSH's focus on worker safety with a focus on environmental health.

Groups mobilized quickly to block this aspect of the Futures Initiative. The American Society of Safety Engineers argued to move NIOSH from the CDC to the Department of Labor (Inside OSHA, 2004b) – a position also argued by the American Industrial Hygiene Association (Harrell, 2004). In August 2004, Gerberding met with a coalition of labor, industry, and safety associations to argue that folding NIOSH into a coordinating center would provide it with more (not fewer) resources; the coalition responded that it would violate the statutory mandate that made NIOSH independent. As was noted the unified position for both labor and industry in this meeting: "These people don't usually agree. It is significant" (quoted in Inside OSHA, 2004c).

Events spiraled, leading to letters against the reorganization signed "by every NIOSH Director back to the Nixon administration and by assistant secretaries for labor and health from both Republican and Democratic administrations" (Weiss, 2004, A19). One concern about this part of the Futures Initiative – and one reason why Gerberding's views were not always heeded – was Kent Nelson's involvement given his past opposition to ergonomics standards (Weiss, 2004; Woodhouse, 2004).

Gerberding countered by offering a $1 million increase in the NIOSH research budget (Inside OSHA, 2004d). The tactical change was judged hollow: "Among the rank and file it's business as usual, but not at the top and none of this [Gerberding's actions] can change the fact that NIOSH is losing a lot of ground" (quoted in Inside OSHA, 2004d).

The Senate responded by attaching language to the FY 2005 Labor, HHS, and Education spending bill prohibiting reducing NIOSH's budget and retaining its direct report relationship with the CDC Director (Inside OSHA, 2004e). The CDC proceeded with folding NIOSH into a coordinating center, although now confronted by the new "Friends of NIOSH" created by the AFL-CIO, the National Mining Association, and others (Inside OSHA, 2004f). After the bill passed the conference committee, the CDC announced that it would not move NIOSH into a coordinating center, but NIOSH budget personnel would now report to the CDC instead of NIOSH (Inside OSHA, 2004h). For two weeks, there was uncertainty as to whether the CDC would follow the Congressional directive (Inside OSHA, 2004g). In truth, NIOSH had already moved to the coordinating center; Gerberding had to rescind the transfer to satisfy Congress.

The degree of opposition to the plan was substantial: "Never before have organized labor, industry, professionals come together like this. Congress saw how important it was to the health and safety community and acted" (an organized labor official quoted in Inside OSHA, 2004g).

This simmered for a long time, partly because Gerberding omitted the NIOSH Director from the Executive Leadership Board and transferred funds and staff from NIOSH to the CDC (Inside OSHA, 2005b). Later, proposals emerged to move NIOSH to the NIH or the Department of Labor (Inside OSHA, 2005a).

This shows the two-sided nature of involving outside partners in deliberative goal setting. Managers at the CDC saw efficiency and accountability benefits from locating NIOSH in a coordinating center, but their partners (representing scientific and technical interests) wanted a protected position for NIOSH in the CDC. These partners formed an "unholy" coalition so NIOSH would not be treated as another center within the agency. It is notable that professionals like safety engineers and industrial hygienists sought to move NIOSH from the CDC and that Nelson's involvement also influenced this debate.

Professional associations and interest groups can intervene in structural manipulation if they see structure as directly affecting their interests and autonomy in policy formulation and implementation. This "politics of bureaucratic structure" operates even if members of Congress or other affected interests are largely ignorant of the dimensions of change (Moe, 1989). NIOSH seems minor given the larger plans and their potential for improving public health capacity, but groups associated with science and engineering professionals and others saw these changes as important enough to act.

The Tyranny of Small Events

The 2004 GAO report was justified by numerous ongoing investigations about financial reporting and accountability concerns at the CDC; it was subsequently used to justify conclusions about the need for reorganizing the CDC. Scandal is a common motivator for reorganizing public agencies (March & Olson, 1983; Moe, 1991), but how people make sense of an organizational change event partly depends on any hints of trouble accompanying the event. The tyranny of small events is that positive interpretations of reorganization can die by a thousand cuts.

For instance, in mid-2006, CDC employees learned that employees in functions like budgeting, accounting, and information technology earned the highest bonuses. Data showed that scientists were few of the seventy-two staffers receiving bonuses of $2,500 or more from 2000 through mid-2006, even though they represented most of the agency's workforce. Members of the Senior Executive Service (SES) are eligible for bonuses of up to 12 percent of salary;

in 2006, the CDC had thirty members of the SES in its ranks (Young, 2006d). Bill Gimson himself received the largest bonuses – $147,863 from mid-2002 to mid-2006, including the Presidential Rank Award and another for distinguished service. (Gimson argued that many bonuses handed out were associated with the agency's implementation of a new accounting system.) As noted, few awards went to actual scientists; the largest award for a scientist went to the head of the division of sexually transmitted disease prevention.

CDC spokesman Glen Nowak responded by saying that "If we want to retain people, we need to recognize them. We are operating in a highly competitive environment" (Harris, 2006), and the president's Management Agenda for the improvement of budgeting and technology did not offer an opportunity for rewarding those on the science side (Young, 2006d). Gerberding responded by naming CDC CFO Barbara Harris to co-chair a panel investigating bonuses; Harris herself received $88,394 in bonuses from 2000 to 2006 (Young, 2006c). Many anonymous comments appeared on the CDC Chatter blog about the distribution of bonuses – and received play in newspaper coverage. The bonuses became a basis for Congressional investigations, including a report entitled "how an agency tasked with fighting and preventing disease has spent hundreds of millions of tax dollars for failed prevention efforts, international junkets, and lavish facilities, but cannot demonstrate it is controlling disease" (United States Senate Subcommittee on Federal Financial Management, Government Information, and International Security, Minority Office, 2007).

Other events also shaped the perceptions of employees within the organization and partners outside the organization about the overall effectiveness of reorganization. For instance, GAO investigated a whistleblower's allegation of poor oversight of the impact of billions of dollars of bioterrorism preparedness grants to the states (U.S. Government Accountability Office, 2002). The HHS Office of the Inspector General investigated whistleblower allegations of altered or falsified payments to pharmaceutical companies (Young, 2006e). Other concerns emerged about problems in the CDC's financial management office (Young, 2006g). In 2006, the media obtained a 2005 CDC self-study of its performance during and after Hurricane Katrina that the CDC initially refused to release to the public or Congressional investigators (Young, 2006h, 2006j).

Yet, most of these "scandals" about "control" and "accountability" occurred among the management functions, not among scientists – which resulted in even greater tensions with the scientists who saw reform as reducing their autonomy. A final notable event came in December 2006 when senior leadership struggled to explain a contract written without competition for $10 million in consulting business with Celerant Consulting; Celerant helped overhaul the CDC's procurement and grants office from 2003 to 2005. An internal CDC public relations risk management analysis called the contract a significant procurement mistake, noting that a contract had been "inappropriately back-dated" (Young, 2006i). Celerant was recommended by James W. Down, a volunteer business advisor to Gerberding and a member of the CDC Foundation board of directors; Down was also negotiating to join Celerant's advisory board. News media noted that Kent Nelson, a reorganization advisor, had introduced Gerberding to Down. HHS issued a stop-work order in 2004 after Celerant was hired on an IT contract with NIH but then allowed the CDC to reinstate the contract (by backdating). As a result, senators requested a GAO inquiry.

The 2004 GAO study argued that the CDC needed clear and effective financial controls, as well as other mechanisms for insuring accountability. The CDC answered with the Futures Initiative and other financial changes. Yet, small events like these affected the reorganization process. External stake-holders and Congress saw missteps that amplified existing concerns about what leaders and managers wanted and how their plans affected the morale of the CDC's scientific core. These events also shaped CDC employees' perceptions about a reorganization many distrusted from the start because it emphasized customers, business processes, and control – when most of the problems seemed to be on the side of management and not among the scientific core.

These events also reinforced beliefs about the way reorganization changed the routines and processes that determined how people do their jobs. The lack of clear and effective financial controls makes life difficult in matrix organizations. Interviews with senior personnel indicated that it was difficult to staff positions because the agency lacked accounting and communications software to help people work in collaborative teams. It also was made difficult due to the nature of federal funding mechanisms for specific programs. For much of that time, the agency lacked the ability to allocate work hours for accurate accounting, necessary for committing individuals to the matrix work teams. Other notorious problems were an HHS-mandated communications system and a travel man-agement system. Without such systems in place, the matrix was seen as an overwhelming burden by professionals more interested in public health science.

Morale Suffered

Soon after reorganization began, conversations started within and outside the CDC about whether the reorganization process was damaging the morale of careerists within the agency and whether that damage had caused the loss of senior staff with significant technical expertise and experience. Unlike the debate over the NIOSH, which mostly subsided, the debate about morale became a central focus of stakeholders outside the CDC and leaders within the organization.

My focus is on how information about potential morale problems made its way from inside the agency to stakeholders (like Congressional committees) outside the agency. To a degree, in focusing on the transit of information and perceptions, it is less important whether the statements of current and former employees, or the views of senior leadership, were accurate or representative. This is because those statements shaped the prospects for the Director in implementing such a major strategic reform effort.

One of the first hints that the Futures Initiative might be causing dissension at the CDC came in February 2005, two months before the announcement of the final design but a year into the planning process. The CDC faced the prospect of significant budget cuts, and the agency had experienced cuts the prior year. This possibility was reported as adding to a malaise caused by the loss of long-term staff to retirements over the previous eighteen months, especially because some retirements occurred before employees faced mandatory retirement deadlines. Half of the center directorships were open, and numerous other positions created in the reorganization remained empty (Wahlberg & McKenna, 2005).

Later, a high-profile news article in the *Washington Post* reported growing internal dissension as a result of the concentration of work time and effort on the Futures Initiative; media reported that forty top managers departed due to dissatisfaction (and eligibility for retirement), the prospect of budget cuts of $500 million, and perceptions of political interference in science at the agency (Stein, 2005). Bob Keegan, formerly of the Global Immunization Program, then recently retired, noted a "crisis of confidence" and that people felt "cowed into silence."

Some said that the process had been "open, inclusive, and positive" and that "we'll get through this difficult period of change and end up in a situation where we're concentrating on our job, which is to protect people's health" (Stein, 2005). They saw the loss of senior scientists as "an opportunity to bring in newer and younger people. It's healthy sometimes to get new people with new ideas" (Stein, 2005). Yet, others argued that "The CDC is our thin gray line when it comes to public health" (Alfred Sommer, Dean of the Johns Hopkins Bloomberg School of Public Health, quoted in Stein, 2005).

More importantly, that media coverage shifted attention away from the reorganization itself (as seen in the debate over NIOSH) to reorganization's impact on the agency's capacity to protect public health. A number of people, including those interviewed for this Element, voiced concern that reorganization damaged capacity for responding to public health crises given the loss of scientists with leadership experience gained post-9/11.

This accelerated with growing concern about science in agencies during the Bush Administration, given debates about research projects on topics ranging from sexually transmitted diseases (STDs) to global warming, undertaken by agencies like the CDC, the NIH, the Environmental Protection Agency, and the National Oceanic and Atmospheric Administration. In 2004, the American Public Health Association adopted policy statement 200411 "Threats to Public Health Science" that broadly indicted the move in the Administration and elsewhere to undervalue the role of science, to weaken science professions, and to categorize traditional science professions as "junk science" through the call for "sound science" (American Public Health Association, 2004). In September 2006, engineers and scientists, including two Nobel Prize winners, created Scientists and Engineers for America to oppose a "bad policy" of political interference in the scientific enterprise in public agencies (Nesmith, 2006). The group specifically described frustration of scientists at the CDC as a primary example of the kind of "bad policy" they were opposing.

As individuals left the CDC, they sometimes described to outsiders (especially journalists) their perception of a lack of support for science in the agency. For instance, in an interview given by John Santelli, a former STD researcher at the CDC who left for Columbia University, he argued, "You want an environment of open inquiry, but you see policy driven more by ideology than science. It was becoming increasingly difficult to do good science in the federal system. The CDC wasn't being as bold as it could in looking at issues that should have been explored" (Abraham, 2005).

Internal survey results in early 2005 echoed a broad concern about how CDC employees saw their contribution to the agency's public health efforts. Two-thirds of employees said that they did not support the Futures Initiative, and less than two-thirds reported that they thought the CDC was improving the health of Americans (a drop of over ten points in two years; Wahlberg, 2005). Less than half responded that CDC could change to meet future challenges, again a drop from two years earlier; 20 percent reported they saw increased opportunities at the CDC (down from 31). Gerberding responded saying that the poll was "done at the worst possible moment as far as people's anxiety."

By 2006, the Senate Finance Committee began an investigation into whether the Futures Initiative was "resulting in the loss of distinguished medical experts whose participation will be greatly needed in the event of future catastrophic health emergencies" (committee spokeswoman Jill Kozeny, quoted in Young, 2006a). CDC leadership disputed the claims, saying that the level of resignations was at a six-year low. This investigation was paired with an announced investigation of a CDC whistleblower's claim that even though the agency had distributed billions of dollars in bioterrorism defense grants to the states, the agency lacked data for assessing the preparedness of local agencies. CDC employees reported that senior management had "consistently rejected or rewritten" measurement tools even though they lacked scientific expertise to judge the tools' merit (Young, 2006a).

By September 2006, the debate was elevated when five former CDC directors sent a joint letter to Director Gerberding noting their "great concern" about the exodus of senior managers and scientists from the agency. They noted that by the end of 2006, all but two of the directors of the eight main CDC centers had left the agency. Director Gerberding countered that she "didn't know any organization that's gone through significant change where morale hasn't been an issue" (Young, 2006b). Her response was to hire an agency-wide ombudsman for responding to criticism (discussed more later).

Morale suffered in part due to a perception of loss of technical expertise; retirements for a category of scientists were 77 percent higher than in previous years (Young, 2006b). Those losses, it was argued, were connected to both the process of reorganization as well as organizational changes brought about by the process. For Stephen Ostroff, a former deputy director of the NCID:

> The sense I get is a lot of the decision-making and a lot of the resources are getting moved away from the scientific underpinnings of the agency. I think there really is the potential for lots of people to take their eye off the ball because they're so heavily engaged in so many of these other things going on in the agency: the reorganization and goals management (Young, 2006b).

In 2007, Don Kettl wrote about Gerberding's management of the CDC's anthrax response and her attempt to reform the agency (Kettl, 2007). Yet, when he was asked about high-profile departures and a loss of morale, he suggested there was trouble ahead, saying "Can you spell FEMA? It's the same kind of issue that they faced" (Kettl, quoted in Young, 2006b). Former senior managers suggested that those inside "don't trust Julie and Bill. It's a reality that the leadership is aware of ... everybody is just befuddled about how you fix that" (Dixie Snider, former CDC chief science officer, quoted in Young, 2006b). Likewise, employees reverting to using blogs to discuss frustrations meant "the commonly accepted avenues of internal communication have either lost their credibility, or broken down completely" (Carlos Alonso, health communication specialist, quoted in Young, 2006b). The CDC responded "what you have is a real mixture of opinions depending on who you speak to and where they are in their career trajectory. I can see why we need to change, but that rationale for change may not have been articulated clearly enough or widely enough or repeatedly enough to sink in" (Kevin Fenton, Director of the National Center for HIV, Sexually Transmitted Diseases, and Tuberculosis, quoted in Young, 2006b).

Congressional committees investigated these media reports; Representative Henry Waxman set up an anonymous tip line for CDC employees to offer insight about the reorganization process (Young, 2006e, 2006g); Representatives created the Congressional Study Group on Public Health to investigate the CDC (Nesmith & Young, 2007). Again, the continuing concern was that a loss of key scientists left the agency unable to respond in a crisis. Keegan noted that "Management has said they've enacted better emergency standards, but until there's an emergency, you don't know" (quoted in Gorman & Fulton, 2006). In January 2007, Lonnie King, the director of the National Center for Zoonotic, Vector-Borne, and Enteric Diseases, sent a memo reporting interviews with over 100 employees that said, "There is frustration, anger, and a sense of things spinning out of control ... The intensity of emotions and commonality of experience across ZVED is both profound and real" (quoted in Young, 2007d). Kettl commented, "Any restructuring will have its growing pains but, in time, there ought to be movement toward the objective. King suggests that things are moving in the opposite direction" (quoted in Young, 2007d). In turn, Senator Grassley noted that when he and Gerberding met and discussed morale in March 2006, she "responded by denying the existence of morale problems at CDC."

How effective was the strategic response to hire two ex-CDC senior officials as independent contractors to serve as ombudsmen? Hired for $250,000 for one year, the ombudsmen spent much of the first three months on the job gathering information about how other ombudsman programs worked at agencies like the NIH, the FDA, and the Tennessee Valley Authority. The one-year contract specifically required the ombudsmen to study and make recommendations about how a permanent ombudsman office should be established (Young, 2007a). In the first three months, they reported receiving and attempting to resolve twenty-six inquiries (Young, 2007b). In response to their efforts, Senator Grassley requested a meeting with the ombudsmen to ask about their role in improving the morale of CDC's employees (Young, 2007c). In March 2007, Gerberding refused that meeting, causing Grassley to respond with a letter detailing the laws about interfering with a congressional investigation: "Dr. Gerberding, am I missing something here? Why would two individuals claim preserving their objectivity as Ombudsmen requires refusing to brief Congress, but allows meeting with you to discuss their findings?" He added that clearly few employees "felt comfortable approaching these two men to seek their help on their problems with CDC management" (Young, 2007e). By April 2007, only ninety-eight inquiries had reached the desk of the ombudsmen, and the ombudsmen had continued to refuse to meet Senator Grassley while continuing to brief Gerberding (Young, 2007f).

In March 2007, Gerberding testified in front of Congress about the issue of morale problems but argued that the main issue was that the agency was now understaffed due to new federal requirements for screening new employees (with 800 people in the queue; Dart, 2007). She had made similar claims in October 2006 during a rare media interview, saying "There isn't a 'brain drain' at CDC. I really do have to object to that characterization. The data do not demonstrate a brain drain. And what you don't talk about is the brain gain. We have a very exciting new generation of great scientists and great leaders coming into CDC" (Young, 2006f). Yet, neither claim seemed to remove much pressure. In April 2007, the five former directors of the CDC reunited for a rare public discussion (held at George Washington University) to argue that at the CDC, science was under fire, just as at the FDA or the Environmental Protection Agency (EPA), and that morale, retention, and recruitment of scientists were in serious jeopardy (Nesmith, 2007). David Satcher, CDC Director from 1993 to 1998, noted that he had "been reluctant to criticize Julie, but I think that a lot of the senior people who left were unhappy about the way it was reorganized" (quoted in Nesmith, 2007).

One high-profile loss in 2007 was the temporary (four-month) assignment of COO Bill Gimson to a Provincial Reconstruction Team in Iraq (later extended until May 2008). At the time, the change was heralded as important in many ways for the CDC; Jeff Levi, executive director of the Trust for America's Health, claimed, "This is a major change for the organization. This is the person who makes the trains run on time. It is the person who translates the director's vision and policy goals" (Young, 2007g). Of course, Gimson was also a primary architect of the Futures Initiative.

Discussion

This section considered three ways of viewing reactions to these strategic changes at the CDC – reactions of people both inside and outside the CDC and how they perceived what leaders brought to the CDC. I focused on critical events that helped define why some people were so dissatisfied with the organization and its operations.

Leaders help organizations make sense of complex environments and action landscapes. They are especially important because, in change environments, individuals interpret events differently as the change process unfolds. However, rather than viewing resistances "not as obstacles to overcome, but as inherent elements of the cognitive transition occurring during change" (Isabella, 1990, 34), the data described here seem to point in a different direction – that CDC employees used critical events and their own experiences in the "new CDC" to form impressions about the capacity of its leaders to implement the Futures Initiative's complex design. In this view, what matters was not leaders "fixing" the reactions, but instead seeing how people came to question the terms of change.

Indeed, how line and staff reacted to critical events should provide a basis for understanding what we actually mean when we say "morale" is low. At a minimum, these three vignettes help show how perceptions and morale related dynamically to the change process. In the next section, data help show that morale and exit are different for different people.

5 Data on the Views of Employees

This section offers a data-driven approach to understanding organizational dissatisfaction at the CDC in the wake of the reorganization effort. In February 2007, the US Office of Personnel Management released its biennial Federal Human Capital Survey (FHCS), widely recognized as the most accurate representation of attitudes toward work and organization among federal employees. These data were quickly examined and debated, with the common interpretation that the CDC was in trouble. CDC senior leaders did little to dissuade these interpretations. Director Gerberding argued in an email that "Some may be tempted to 'spin' the information from this survey in either a positive way or a negative way, or claim that it is 'outdated,' 'not representative,' 'not scientific,' or 'incomplete,' but I'd like to set aside those concerns. I believe that we should just take it at face value" (Shoop, 2007).

The previous section suggests that issues about morale within the organization became the basis for interpretations of why senior people were leaving the organization. These interpretations, when combined with the views of stakeholders outside the organization and those of former senior CDC staff, supported increasing scrutiny of the CDC, its reorganization, and the leadership qualities of senior staff. In the process, the media amplified these interpretations, along conversations occurring in other venues like blogs. That scrutiny brought about the use of ombudsmen, although the implementation of that strategy itself caused additional scrutiny.

The FHCS data in this section offer a more accurate representation of rank-and-file views of whether morale and turnover were problems at the CDC with the Futures Initiative. The focus here is on individual-level interpretations for line and staff. How different were the CDC employees' responses from other employees within the HHS? The FHCS measures the perceptions of employees about the conditions of the organizations they work in. Now known as the Federal Employee Viewpoint Survey, this then-biennial survey was first administered in 2002. US Office of Personnel Management (OPM) uses the survey to obtain general indicators of human resources management systems in federal agencies, to assess agencies regarding the strategic management of human capital, and (most importantly) to provide senior managers with information about how they can make their agencies work better (U.S. Office of Personnel Management, 2020). The data are stratified to be demographically representative and so are useful for making accurate inferences about work conditions; for individual orientations toward co-workers, supervisors, and senior leadership; and for assessing other matters like the likelihood of retirement or turnover.

Specifically, the data were collected from survey respondents and then adjusted to be representative of the underlying population of federal employees; the data I obtain from this process are weighted. The weight indicates how many employees in the federal employee population that a given respondent represents; weights are developed using information about demographics like gender, race, supervisory status, age, and agency size. Not weighting data makes it difficult to generalize from the survey respondents to the population. These data were weighted in three steps based on the employee's probability of selection, survey nonresponse, and the use of known information about the survey population.

In interpreting the results that follow, it is important to recall the timing of the data. Released in 2007, these results postdate many of the first reactions to the reform effort. Indeed, most of the investigations about high-profile resignations and retirements already were underway. This dampens the observed impact of the reform effort as measured at the individual level.[5]

Tables 1–4 present four views of the perceptions of individuals within the CDC of their organization and the people they work with. For each comparison, I tabulated the responses for each question for individuals within the CDC and compared them with the responses for each question for all individuals working within HHS who do not work for the CDC. This provides a within-department comparison with the treatment variable being the location of an employee within the CDC. Were the CDC employees' perceptions really that different from other employees within HHS? Of course, the comparison is not perfect, but it does help illuminate whether the CDC experience was unique within the overall framework of the US public health organizational infrastructure.

Table 3 starts with a comparison of respondents with regard to the statement "The people I work with cooperate to get the job done." The responses show that

---

[5] Recognizing the need for timely data, the US Office of Personnel Management now administers government-wide "federal employee voice" pulse surveys every two months to assess topics like employee engagement and inclusion (Coleman, 2021).

Table 3 Employee Viewpoints

Group	Strongly Disagree	Disagree	Neither Agree nor Disagree	Agree	Strongly Agree
The people I work with cooperate to get the job done.					
Other HHS (%)	1.64	6.25	8.80	53.13	30.19
CDC (%)	1.45	5.94	9.45	51.74	31.42
Creativity and innovation are rewarded.					
Agency	Strongly Disagree	Disagree	Neither Agree nor Disagree	Agree	Strongly Agree
Other HHS (%)	10.88	17.01	27.58	31.26	9.98
CDC (%)	10.74	19.03	26.66	32.34	8.63
I recommend my organization as a good place to work.					
Agency	Strongly Disagree	Disagree	Neither Agree nor Disagree	Agree	Strongly Agree
Other HHS (%)	5.98	9.18	20.92	40.11	23.80
CDC (%)	7.20	13.17	22.30	37.66	19.67
I know how my work relates to the agency's goals and priorities.					
Agency	Strongly Disagree	Disagree	Neither Agree nor Disagree	Agree	Strongly Agree
Other HHS (%)	1.73	3.09	9.70	54.42	30.34
CDC (%)	3.21	7.23	13.10	52.54	22.92
Employees have a feeling of personal empowerment with respect to work processes.					
Agency	Strongly Disagree	Disagree	Neither Agree nor Disagree	Agree	Strongly Agree
Other HHS (%)	8.58	16.03	28.46	36.12	7.37
CDC (%)	10.94	21.24	28.45	31.35	5.12

How satisfied are you with your involvement in decisions that affect your work?

Agency	Strongly Disagree	Disagree	Neither Agree nor Disagree	Agree	Strongly Agree
Other HHS (%)	6.05	16.92	22.27	41.75	13.01
CDC (%)	8.73	22.13	22.19	36.55	10.40

Promotions in my work unit are based on merit.

Agency	Strongly Disagree	Disagree	Neither Agree nor Disagree	Agree	Strongly Agree
Other HHS (%)	12.74	15.58	25.65	30.05	8.92
CDC (%)	15.65	19.40	23.60	29.15	6.76

CDC employees were slightly less likely to respond "strongly disagree" and slightly more likely to respond "strongly agree." Clearly, this attribute of the CDC work environment was not the source of the morale problems discussed previously. CDC employees were slightly less likely to respond "strongly disagree" and slightly more likely to respond "agree" with regard to the statement "Creativity and innovation are rewarded." Interestingly, there is a two-point difference in the case of "disagree," with CDC employees more likely to disagree with the statement about the reward of creativity and innovation.

The second half of Table 3 shows several differences, though. CDC employees were more likely to respond "agree" or "strongly disagree" with the statement "I recommend my organization as a good place to work." The same holds for the statement "I know how my work relates to the agency's goals and priorities"; note that in this case, CDC employees were almost eight points lower in responding "strongly agree." This pattern holds for the statements "Employees have a feeling of personal empowerment with regard to work processes," "How satisfied are you with your involvement in decisions that affect your work?" and "Promotions in my work unit are based on merit."

Each of these items in Table 3 was selected because they relate to the respondent's general orientation toward the organization or their co-workers. And together they show that CDC employees were more likely to be dissatisfied with these aspects of the workplace than other HHS employees.

Table 4 turns to the employee's relationship with hierarchical authorities. The differences are small with regard to the statement "Arbitrary action, personal favoritism, and coercion for partisan political purposes are not tolerated." What is useful about this item is that it gets at the common complaint that the CDC's leaders are acting in a political way. The data from the FHCS seem to indicate otherwise: CDC employees were not relatively more likely to see supervisors in this way than other employees at HHS although almost 25 percent of respondents in both organizations still see such actions as being tolerated. From this point on, we see more separation between the responses for the CDC employees and the others in HHS. The differences are small in the case of "Supervisors/team leaders in my work unit provide employees with opportunities to demonstrate their leadership skills," but CDC employees' responses were more negative as we move from an item about trust to one about progress toward goals/objectives to two about the how leaders communicate the organization goals and priorities, as well as what is generally going on.

For these items, we see that responses were relatively more negative in the case of the CDC than those from the rest of HHS as we move from questions about partisan control to questions about information provision. One inference

Table 4 Employee Viewpoints

Agency	Strongly Disagree	Disagree	Neither Agree nor Disagree	Agree	Strongly Agree
Arbitrary action, personal favoritism, and coercion for partisan political purposes are not tolerated.					
Other HHS (%)	11.39	11.24	24.64	30.45	12.57
CDC (%)	11.52	13.43	25.14	29.25	11.09
Supervisors/team leaders in my work unit provide employees with opportunities to demonstrate their leadership skills.					
Agency	Strongly Disagree	Disagree	Neither Agree nor Disagree	Agree	Strongly Agree
Other HHS (%)	6.09	10.79	20.87	40.77	20.39
CDC (%)	6.98	12.98	19.60	39.25	20.19
I have trust and confidence in my supervisor.					
Agency	Strongly Disagree	Disagree	Neither Agree nor Disagree	Agree	Strongly Agree
Other HHS (%)	7.47	9.70	17.48	35.43	29.91
CDC (%)	8.45	10.94	17.06	35.48	28.07
Managers review and evaluate the organization's progress toward meeting its goals and objectives.					
Agency	Strongly Disagree	Disagree	Neither Agree nor Disagree	Agree	Strongly Agree
Other HHS (%)	5.19	8.52	24.39	44.17	12.16
CDC (%)	6.79	12.03	28.41	38.81	7.05
Managers communicate the goals and priorities of the organization.					
Agency	Strongly Disagree	Disagree	Neither Agree nor Disagree	Agree	Strongly Agree
Other HHS (%)	6.97	11.29	21.97	45.88	12.58
CDC (%)	8.78	14.49	25.86	42.15	7.57

Table 4 (cont.)

Agency	Strongly Disagree	Disagree	Neither Agree nor Disagree	Agree	Strongly Agree

How satisfied are you with the information you receive from management on what's going on in your organization?

Agency	Strongly Disagree	Disagree	Neither Agree nor Disagree	Agree	Strongly Agree
Other HHS (%)	8.43	20.09	25.03	36.84	9.62
CDC (%)	11.60	25.10	23.56	32.95	6.80

here is that CDC employees were relatively more sensitive about information flows from the top of the organization to the bottom, with 36 percent of respondents voicing negative impressions of that flow. This is worth noting because matrix forms are better at moving information up the hierarchy than they are at moving information down. Employee perceptions reflect this aspect of matrix management.

Table 5 moves inward again and asks whether respondents were likely to leave or retire soon. Interestingly, Table 3 shows that CDC employees were significantly more likely to say they are not leaving in the next year, although those who were leaving are more likely to respond that they are leaving to retire. From a human capital perspective, clearly, there were issues at HHS, and for the CDC, the issues were mostly centered around retirement issues. Almost a third were planning to take another job within the federal government, but mobility to which other organization is difficult to assess in the context of this survey. A quarter of CDC employees said they planned to take a job outside the federal government, but again this number was lower than for those in the rest of HHS.

Table 5 also looks at the pace of planned retirement. CDC employees were less likely to retire within the next year and slightly more likely to respond they would retire in five or more years. On its face, the data seem to indicate little obvious reason for concern about retirements at the CDC. There are two hidden possibilities, though. The first is that the important retirements occurred before this survey was administered. That is possible, but not testable. The second is that the likelihood of retiring (or leaving generally) varied with rank. Analysis by rank shows no major differences for the leaving item, except that supervisors at the CDC were about twice as likely to leave for another job outside the federal government; that level, though, was still less than 10 percent of the supervisory workforce. The main difference by rank is instead for planned retirements. The data show that almost a quarter of the SES class of its equivalent planned to retire in the next one to three years – and that number is 50 percent higher than the same incidence for the rest of HHS.

Table 6 presents four items that address leaders and employees' perceptions of them at the CDC and HHS. CDC employees were consistently more negative about their leaders than other employees at HHS. The levels are also striking. A third of employees disagreed or strongly disagreed with the statement that "I have a high level of respect for my organization's leaders"; that number was 30 percent higher than that for other HHS employees. Almost 40 percent of CDC employees disagreed or strongly disagreed with the statement that they were satisfied with the policies and practices of senior leaders; 25 percent agreed and only 5 percent strongly agreed. Over 40 percent disagreed or

Table 5 Employee Viewpoints

Are you considering leaving your organization within the next year, and if so, why?

Agency	No	Yes, to retire	Yes, to take another job within the federal government	Yes, to take another job outside the federal government	Yes, other
Other HHS (%)	9.61	18.49	30.16	32.80	8.94
CDC (%)	16.11	23.73	29.31	25.31	5.54

I am planning to retire.

Agency	Within one year	Between one and three years	Between three and five years	Five or more years
Other HHS (%)	3.33	9.49	10.07	77.11
CDC (%)	2.62	7.56	11.10	78.72

Table 6 Employee Viewpoints

Agency	Strongly Disagree	Disagree	Neither Agree nor Disagree	Agree	Strongly Agree
My organization's leaders maintain high standards of honesty and integrity.					
Other HHS (%)	9.52	10.91	25.97	34.41	14.89
CDC (%)	13.24	13.23	28.85	29.71	10.51
In my organization, leaders generate high levels of motivation and commitment in the workforce.					
Agency	Strongly Disagree	Disagree	Neither Agree nor Disagree	Agree	Strongly Agree
Other HHS (%)	11.50	18.39	28.36	29.80	10.48
CDC (%)	17.43	23.67	27.40	23.67	6.62
How satisfied are you with the policies and practices of your senior leaders?					
Agency	Strongly Disagree	Disagree	Neither Agree nor Disagree	Agree	Strongly Agree
Other HHS (%)	9.61	18.49	30.16	32.80	8.94
CDC (%)	16.11	23.73	29.31	25.31	5.54
I have a high level of respect for my organization's senior leaders.					
Agency	Strongly Disagree	Disagree	Neither Agree nor Disagree	Agree	Strongly Agree
Other HHS (%)	10.04	12.89	23.35	35.96	16.93
CDC (%)	16.78	16.78	24.88	29.73	11.10

strongly disagreed that leaders generate high levels of motivation and commitment in the workforce.

The difficulty with perceptions is that they are individual while being
observed in a social world. A cohort of employees at the CDC clearly held
negative perceptions of their leaders. Those perceptions were significantly more
negative than those of employees in other HHS agencies. The measurement of
these perceptions postdates the most conflictual parts of the reform process (the
time when the most high-profile exits occurred). Just as individual perceptions
depend on news and events from the organization within which they reside, so
too are they affected by the number of people in the organization voicing
negative perceptions. The real danger at the CDC was not that people were
negative or that they do not see the benefits of the Futures Initiative – it is that
they learned how negative their co-workers were on average and then they
would decide they should be even more negative. The real risk was the
downward spiral.

6 Conclusion: Herding Scientists

On January 20, 2009, as Barack Obama began his first term, Julie Gerberding
resigned as Director of the CDC. Newly returned from Iraq, COO Bill Gimson
served as interim until Tom Frieden took the helm (serving from 2009 to 2017).
Within a short time, almost all the changes started under Gerberding were gone.
As one reporter described the situation, "No federal health agency changed
more during the Bush administration than the CDC. It got new buildings, new
managers, and an entirely new operating structure. A year into the Obama
administration, only the new buildings remain." Frieden used a "big broom"
to sweep away all the changes Gerberding spent six years devising and implementing. Instead of nonscientific managers and bureaucracy, Frieden "restored
not only much of the agency's previous organizational structure and scientific
managers, but also its drab furniture." Gone were the Coordinating Centers,
removing a layer between the leaders and the scientists. The journalist noted
"Agency employees and former leaders said in interviews that they were thrilled
with Dr. Frieden's changes" (Harris, 2010).

What can we take away from the CDC's experience with strategic reorganization in its Futures Initiative? Are the experiences so unique to the CDC that
they provide no information about other agencies, in other circumstances,
facing other constraints? What does this set of experiences tell us about how
we herd scientists through reorganization?

It is easy to revert to platitudes like "selecting the right person" or "getting the
structure right" (Abramson & Lawrence, 2001, 8). In this section, I first offer

several small takeaways about the prospects for the management of scientists. After that, I offer a broader observation about the reorganization of large-scale health science organizations. Last, I consider the implications of this narrative for how we think about managerial responses to policy challenges; in that context, I consider how we might think about the future of agencies like CDC given the recent coronavirus pandemic.

The Management of Scientists

First, the CDC's experiences suggest that working with partners can be a rich and rewarding experience. In fact, one may have no choice but to work with partners because not doing so probably dooms reorganization from the outset. Of course, the NIOSH experience shows the unpredictability of outside partners that have their own partners, whose bonds with one another may be stronger than their bonds with the agency. This is especially true when those partners are associations of science professionals.

Indeed, it is impossible to test the counterfactual: What would have happened had the CDC not involved its partners at all? Most likely, the CDC had no choice because public health science depends so much on the use of partners for establishing goals and priorities, as well as carrying out tasks (e.g., public health surveillance).

Since partners are not easily controlled, those wanting to shape public health science organizations are both constrained and enabled by coalitions that form and oppose. In interviews, senior personnel at the CDC constantly emphasized the importance of full, complete, and early communication with stakeholders outside the organization and personnel inside it. NIOSH could have been avoided – if all partners were treated as equals. NIOSH won, and Gerberding lost, but the situation was unstable. Either NIOSH or the Coordinating Centers had to go. In the end, NIOSH survived, supported by its associations. And the Coordinating Centers were gone.

Second, the point of the Coordinating Centers was to enable matrix management. Those organizations aggregate information and refer conflict; they are adept at flexibly identifying opportunities and adapting to rapidly changing external environments. However, they are costly – not all employees have the taste for the kinds of risk that matrix organizations bring with them, and professionalized public employees are notoriously risk-averse (Bellante & Link, 1981; Nicholson-Crotty et al., 2017; Pfeifer, 2011).

Perhaps matrix organizations are not well-suited for the public sector, or maybe it just depends on the application. The problem is that some kinds of employees – perhaps those with rich skillsets, like scientists – are probably loathe to have one direct supervisor, let alone the two or more that some matrix organizations employ. Matrix organizations are predicated on the ability of employees to adapt to environments and different supervisory cultures. Scientists are mostly adaptive, but not always interested in taking on the costs necessary in learning how to navigate a multiple supervisor environment or in building the packages of routines, rules, and procedures that help matrix organizations operate. In the end, the matrix is just a managerial framework (a skeleton) upon which rank-and-file employees have to assemble muscles and skin. However, even firms like ABB have found it difficult to find routines, rules, and procedures that allow the matrix to fully function. In this context, though, herding government scientists makes the problems of matrix even harder to overcome.

Third, the GAO noted in 2004 that the Futures Initiative was too focused on graphical analogs and paid little attention to building strategic human capital. Who can resist working on organization charts when the alternative is making sure that your reform does not trigger a wave of resignations and retirements under conditions of limited funding?

The problem is connected to the costs of putting meat on the bones of organizational change. Reorganization costs are mostly carried by midrange employees, some of whom have survived long enough to make a rational calculation to leave the organization rather than take on the costs of rebuilding an organization that they will likely never see "success" at reorganization (given the five-to-seven-year window argued by the GAO). The previously offered 2007 data suggest there was a crisis of confidence – in top leaders, not peers – but that the CDC's employees who remained were no more likely to leave the organization because of it. Alternatively, those who had not yet resigned or retired may have decided to wait for a likely change in administration (and the change in organizational structure they saw coming).

Fourth, a good chess player can only see twelve moves ahead, and a good game theorist will not even try to do so. NIOSH shows the limits of foresight. It does not mean those events do not matter. In the conceptual framework presented previously, strategic leaders plan out a process of change rooted in goal setting but dependent on getting large numbers of people to change how they do things on an everyday basis. Small events help drive how people perceive the likelihood that the current reform effort will be the one that causes change five years from now. In the CDC context, many of those small events were associated with financial and control scandals connected to with the management side of the agency.

The alternative may be equally compelling: that the small events cause a change in leadership and that change in leadership brings about another planning period that leads to change five years from now. At the CDC, this was clearly the case: the anthrax events lead to Julie Gerberding taking the reins at the CDC, which lead to the Futures Initiative itself. The compilation of small events led to external scrutiny and Congressional investigations; the change of administration and departure of a lame-duck president necessarily brought new leadership.

Fifth, in interviews, senior personnel regularly described the problem of reorganization at the CDC as depending on continuity of leadership. The original GAO admonition to see this change as a five-to-seven-year process was echoed in the comments of personnel, who talked in terms of commitment, persistence, and continuity. The departure of COO Bill Gimson, seen by many as the architect of the Futures Initiative and its primary executor (as well as a primary means for Gerberding to manage the agency), introduced questions about what came next.

The Reorganization Imperative

Many countries use large, complex agencies like the CDC to decide and deliver public health benefits to their national populations. Of course, most of us have little individual understanding of the contours of public health, and collectively, it can be difficult to define public health through public dialogue. While the change seems to be constant across a number of countries, the deliberative setting of goals for reorganizing agencies is a unique and important event in public health. Yet, because the CDC carries substantial weight, how it managed this transformation has important implications for public health debates around the world. The FY 2016 CDC budget request was $11.5 billion (U.S. Department of Health and Human Services, 2015); the FY 2020 budget request was $5.94 billion, with over 10,000 employees facing an ever-growing menu of duties. Just as *Healthy People* focused attention on some health policy problems and away from others, the Futures Initiative plan reshaped debates over national and local public health policies.

At a minimum, the CDC spent six years simply encouraging deliberation about what it should be doing. Knowing the decision's consequences broadens our knowledge of public health, policy debates, and public health bureaucracies large and small. The CDC also understood better the value of goal setting as a policy exercise. Together, these activities enrich our models and expectations for public health science as a political and administrative process, our vision for the collaborative determination of its contours, and our understanding of how agency leaders strategically set goals in order to transform organizational routines, rules, and procedures.

Beyond the walls of the CDC, though, these changes brought two additional and important contributions to public health policy. First, debates over the past three decades about the reform and reorganization of public health policy largely ignored the CDC's considerable footprint. Of course, there is no end to suggestions for what the CDC should be doing at the national, local, and even global levels. What has been missing, though, is a clear understanding of how the CDC tried to reshape itself, the reasons behind those changes, and their consequences for the CDC, its partners, and its customers. The IOM report marked a subtle shift in concentration from what governments are doing to what NGOs can do for governments. This is understandable but regrettable because, while we do not know much about how the CDC has responded to the admonitions of the IOM and others, the CDC remains an inspiration for those organizing solutions to public health problems: both the Canadian Public Health Agency and the European Center for Disease Prevention and Control were modeled roughly on the US CDC.

Second, it can be argued that the CDC's attempted reorganization of its divisions was the most important since the reorganization of Health, Education, and Welfare during the 1960s. The CDC's experiences provide a unique laboratory for understanding that most peculiar American political pastime: reorganization politics. Consider one additional reason for examining the CDC's experience with reform. Draft legislation released by the House Energy and Commerce Committee on July 19, 2005, sought to give the director of the NIH unprecedented authority to (1) select objectives for federal spending and policy for biomedical research and (2) reorganize the NIH's twenty-seven institutes and centers (Weiss, 2005). In 2018, concerns emerged again in the professional science community that President Trump might reorganize NIH (Wilson, 2018). The narrative here provides insight because this wrangling already happened at the CDC. The looming debate about NIH shows that politicians see the same "dizzying array" of agencies, centers, and missions that IOM noted in 1988.

This narrative also tells us something about the design and performance of our highly varied state and local public health systems (Sinclair & Whitford, 2013, 2015). Consider two possible outcomes for the CDC going forward. In the first, the agency becomes less effective and less important on the American public health landscape; in the second, the agency expands its mission as a central organizing force in American public health. In the former case, the organizational change process was either intentionally hollow or insufficient. In the latter, the change process was strategically successful. Some may desire one outcome for normative reasons, but understanding either outcome provides a descriptive assessment of what can happen when we rely on broadly deliberative approaches for goal setting in public organizations – a strategy for which demand seems to be increasing, not decreasing. The health community continues to invest resources in deliberative goal determination, but our best evidence about the performance of those processes in the public health sector is limited to a few isolated cases (Abelson, Eyles, et al., 2003).

Finally, leaders searching for high performance almost always turn to goal setting; strategic visioning is one way to set goals and "fix" large, complex organizations. What can we learn from the strategic transformation of the CDC – accelerated by broad-based deliberation – from a hierarchy to a matrix? Of course, matrix forms are not new, but their broad use in knowledge organizations (like in Silicon Valley) has spread to the government sector. What are the incentives for their use? Certainly, leaders at agencies like the CDC are attracted because tasks are so nonroutine that it is impossible to predict the genesis of the next avian flu, anthrax scare, or other crisis. What is left to answer in these cases, though, is the necessary balance between flexibility, enhanced information sharing, and accountability. Over the long term, what are the costs of such heavy public involvement in the strategic direction of public agencies?

Public Health Science Organizations in the Wake of Coronavirus

Because of our recent and ongoing experiences with coronavirus, governments around the world likely will seek to reform their national, state, and local public health organizations. We know from our long history of studies of reorganization that such attempts create opportunities for improvements in efficiency and effectiveness – and also for reshaping those organizations in the images of those charged with reorganization. In the public health arena, though, the management of science matters more than in other agencies: science organizations are different, and scientists as professionals are different. Science organizations often prove difficult to reform, as evidenced in the attempted reorganization of the US CDC after the 2001 anthrax scare.

Coronavirus has changed the world; coronavirus will continue to change the world. These are now almost platitudes, but as we know well from the world of policy analysis, the devil is always in the details. Over the next decade, thousands of research reports and hundreds of books will be written dissecting what has happened and who is to blame. At this point, it is impossible to fully assess such matters, yet whatever our current judgments, it is almost certain they will be proven wrong over the course of time. One simple reason for this is that the virus itself will evolve, so we are all still very early in this process.

For instance, it is easy to say that coronavirus was anticipated, and it is easy to say that we failed to prepare (Coates, 2019; Fauci, 2017; Morens et al., 2008;

Sun, 2018; Taubenberger et al., 2007). Yet, such judgments are inherently fraught with error. Even if the virus was anticipated, its nature and impact were only forecast with great uncertainty. Similarly, if our forecasts were fundamentally uncertain, sufficient preparation is itself inherently uncertain.

In the United States, it has become clear that political intervention has complicated if not fundamentally damaged the CDC's ability to respond quickly and competently to the coronavirus event. As Jeffrey Koplan, CDC Director during the Clinton and Bush Administrations, put it: "There comes a time when it makes it very hard to operate effectively, when things are being suggested, requested, ordered that you think are contrary to the containment of the pandemic" (Lipton et al., 2020). While attention rightly also has focused on the agency's missteps in handling the novel coronavirus, the agency (like other science agencies) had been the target of political intervention since the beginning of the Trump Administration (Carter, 2019). Some of this might be ascribed to wrangling over turf between agencies like the CDC and the Department of Homeland Security; some of it could be from traditional lobbying efforts by companies (like test manufacturers) clamoring for a piece of the pie (Maxmen & Tollefson, 2020). Maybe it was all just due to a shortsighted political decision to dismantle the White House office for pandemic preparedness. Perhaps that Administration's leadership was just spectacularly inept on coronavirus; as former CDC Directors Tom Frieden, Jeffrey Koplan, David Satcher, and Richard Besser titled their op-ed on this, "We ran the CDC. No president ever politicized its science the way Trump has" (Frieden et al., 2020).

Yet, even if specific countries have differentially "succeeded" in preparation and mitigation so far, we know such judgments are fragile because of our limited knowledge about this pathogen. Will it return? Will it change? What are expected future damages? As David Krakauer noted, in this context, our forecast errors result from the complex causes at play (Krakauer, 2020).

As such, observers will offer a multitude of solutions, each operating on a dimension of a complex policy implementation space, without a clear understanding of how they aggregate across organizations, people, and time – at least until the next event occurs. This is because each event is to a degree a "black swan" (Taleb, 2007); each is unpredictable, consequential, and ex post explainable. If such events were well-anticipated, we could insure against them easily, but the most insurable events do not occur in part because they were well-anticipated. As such, we cannot easily observe the fragilities of such systems against tail risks.

The only thing for certain is that cities, states, nations, and even the international community will seek to reform the public health agencies charged with anticipating and mitigating those tail risks. What guidance can we offer for those future endeavors?

First, we know that politicians and other actors look for windows of opportunity for reshaping agencies; the outcomes of organizations depend on how those windows interact with the incentives of the actors driving for reform. Second, the operations of agencies depend on these incremental changes over time; the "game" is like a chaotic soccer match, where the "slope of the field produces a bias in how the balls fall and what goals are reached" (March & Romelaer, 1976, 276). Third, to an extent more than is usually admitted, reorganization outcomes are driven by competition between administrative and political motives; competing and common symbols drive the outcomes of reorganization.

As such, reorganization itself seems almost like a black swan event. For instance, China's Center for Disease Control (CCDC) is responsible for the surveillance of infectious diseases at the national, provincial, prefectural, and county levels (Vlieg et al., 2017). It now has 70,000 reporting units and includes county-level organizations and most township-level healthcare providers (Ren et al., 2019). While the system was created in 2002, its current organization evolved after the advent of SARS in 2003 (Feng et al., 2011; Lan, 2005). As part of this, China's CDC offices now report information on thirty-nine different infectious diseases (Vlieg et al., 2017). SARS showed how the 2002 creation of China's CDC was a hollow enterprise – afterward, reorganization became a top public policy priority (Li et al., 2016). Just a few short years after CCDC's creation in 2002 and then SARS, China had built a national network of field stations. Indeed, in a very short period of time, the system had evolved from a low-tech network to a "professionalized, biomedicalized, and globalized technology machine" (Mason, 2016, 3).

Judging CCDC's recent response to coronavirus is beyond the scope of this Element; indeed, it is too early to make definitive statements. However, it is easy to see how this reorganization event followed the three observations previously offered. First, reorganization followed SARS. Second, the game of reorganization provided opportunities for knitting together a complex, geographically dispersed population – a longtime ambition. Last, the choice of the label "CDC" is acknowledgment of the historically important creation of the United States' own CDC in 1946.

As far as we can tell, the reform of China's CDC after SARS positively affected its handling of the coronavirus pandemic. It is impossible to fully assess those effects at this point because even if we believe the record as it is currently presented regarding China's response, we will never observe the counterfactual – China's handling of the crisis without those changes in place.

The broader point is that learning from past reorganization attempts helps us better understand the range of possible opportunities, strategies, and missteps when we open an agency's organization for reassembly. Rather than focus on the current situation, I will offer here a viewpoint drawn from the US CDC and its reorganization following events in 2001 in which anthrax was used as a bioterrorism agent. Within two years, the Bush Administration sought a top-to-bottom restructuring of the CDC to improve the national response to such events. In many ways, the CDC's "Futures Initiative" was a failure, but those points of failure tell us something about what follows this current crisis. What can past reorganizations like these tell us as we enter an era where the most likely outcome will be the push to reform the agencies that we trusted to protect us from coronavirus?

Before moving forward, all efforts at reshaping public health science organizations will depend on answers to this question: "What is public health?" Who decides the contours of public health, and what are the organizational consequences of those decisions? Those making these decisions are not engaging in neutral activities; their decisions will have substantial consequences for those science organizations charged with delivering and insuring population-level public health outcomes. Yet, herding scientists is always fraught with risk, if only because we do not know enough about the governance of scientific organizations in traditional policy implementation.

In this Element, I have made four key statements. First, new public problems emerge; politicians and their proxies demand change; and professionals like scientists seek out and advocate for solutions, so "herding" is a core part of the policy process. Second, political appointees use tools like reorganization to "steer the boat" of public scientific organizations, but they also engage with and are shaped by constituencies, stakeholders, and sellers of advice. Third, whatever emerges from the reorganization process helps determine how those agencies do their daily work; those "smaller skirmishes" also affect whether reorganization succeeds. Last, few of the scientists living inside agencies joined to attend to organizational change. At the CDC, morale suffered, and many of the most valuable scientific leaders left the organization.

This reveals a dilemma: policy processes depend on the knowledge and technical expertise of scientists, but their agencies are managed by generalists, who are appointed by politicians. "Shuffling the deck" through reorganization of groups of mostly disinterested scientists constrains the set of possible outcomes. Moreover, the task environment continues to evolve despite the deck shuffling.

Aspects of this are clear enough in the case of China's reorganization: in 2002, China's creation of their agency was meant to lay the groundwork for new ways to solve broad public health programs, yet within the next year, SARS brought about a whole new spate of unforeseen contingencies that engendered new rounds of reorganization. Likewise, at the US CDC, the anthrax events of 2001 led to Gerberding taking the reins because she had served as the public face of the agency's response efforts, and her ascension to the directorship produced the Futures Initiative itself. Which new pathogen or public health threat will dismantle the reorganization now being planned for these public health organizations?

This is the difficulty in reorganization efforts: unless we believe in perfect structures, each reorganization sows the seeds of its own demise. Missed opportunities or overreactions create the organizational fragilities that shape future responses to new threats. We know that there are no neutral organizational structures – each one has its own myopia – but it is hard to know ex ante the myopia being created in current times for future requirements.

This is even harder in the case of science-based organizations like the public health agencies we ask to protect us from current and future pathogenic threats. Like other employees, they live in organizations, not of their own making, but the CDC's experience reveals two special problems that are hard to solve: that we need to hear their views when building the next organization within which they will operate, but that they rarely have strong interests in the nuts and bolts of reorganization. Of course, professionals are all special, but "herding scientists" is an especially difficult enterprise. Even in the case of China, some have argued that their agency focuses too much on science and not enough on traditional solutions to local health problems (Mason, 2016).

Moreover, reorganizing agencies is especially hard when their purpose is to reduce the probability of the next "inconceivable" threat. Notwithstanding the fact that black swans are real and they live in Australia, the broader point is that there are an infinite number of possible existential threats on the horizon. It is improbable that reorganization builds perfect agencies populated by attentive public servants who foresee and mitigate all possible threats. But even so, another round of reorganization will attempt to reduce the errors of the past only at the cost of sowing the seeds of future errors. Removing policy errors is impossible, but it is possible to mitigate them by avoiding strategic reorganization errors.

Herding Scientists

The quest of herding scientists is fraught with uncertainty and missteps. One of the central goals of this story is to help us better understand the tension between scientists and managerial control in complex policymaking organizations, both conceptually and empirically. Reform efforts like the one undertaken here are high-profile strategic efforts to change the overall direction of boatloads of scientists. Clearly, public scientific agencies exist and have operated for centuries (Carpenter, 2001, 2010), so by now people have figured out they are useful, indeed necessary, for making and implementing complex public policies. The character and qualities of scientists have driven researchers to better understand how core public management levers like "red tape" shape the day-to-day operations of government's knowledge organizations (Crow & Bozeman, 1998). Most of the time, politicians have ignored those "black boxes" and the scientists who inhabit them (Crow & Bozeman, 1998, xx).

But sometimes politicians have turned their managerial whims to those agencies, and increasingly politicians see the day-to-day behavior of government scientists as worthy of their attention. In those cases, reform via reorganization is the natural lever to pull because it is what politicians do when they want to shake things up (March & Olson, 1983; Peters, 1992). The story of failed reform at the CDC tells us how hard it is to make that change without damaging the agency's core capacity and comparative abilities. Sometimes politicians deem it necessary to "reboot" an agency (even scientific ones) because they perceive its professionals as beyond redemption (Aron, 1982; Temples, 1982), so we must recognize that even scientists as government employees are not immune from the reform imperative.

The CDC story centers on reorganization because it may be that politicians find that lever easier to pull in a science agency than more traditional levers of control and authority. It may be that generalists and professionals are doomed to a war of attrition, if only because (as Parsons, 1939 noted) scientists long have seen themselves as the preeminent profession. This debate is unlikely to be decided in a single case or country; undoubtedly, even if a silver bullet solution could be found to the problem of managing scientists, clever professionals likely would seek ways to circumvent those controls and again exert their autonomy.

Instead, it is worth our attention to consider what can go wrong when trying to make wholesale changes to an agency following events that some, if not many, perceive as failures by the agency (Gottlieb, 2021; Lewis, 2021; Slavitt, 2021). Failed reorganization does not invalidate the call for reform, but it does suggest that true reform is much harder to attain than most expect. But each new reform effort is a legacy of past failures more than successes, so knowledge about those failures can only aid in the herding of scientists via reorganization.

Acronyms and Abbreviations

ATSDR:	Agency for Toxic Substances and Disease Registry
CDC:	Centers for Disease Control and Prevention
CFO:	chief financial officer
CIO:	chief information officer
CMO:	chief management official
COO:	chief operating officer
CSO:	chief science officer
FHCS:	Federal Human Capital Survey
GAO:	Government Accountability Office
HHS:	Department of Health and Human Services
NCID:	National Center for Infectious Diseases
NIH:	National Institutes of Health
OD:	Office of the Director
OSHA:	Occupational Safety and Health Administration
OTPER:	Office of Terrorism Preparedness and Emergency Response
PHS:	Public Health Service
SARS:	severe acute respiratory syndrome

References

Abelson, J., Eyles, J., McLeod, C. B. et al. (2003). Does Deliberation Make a Difference? Results from a Citizens Panel Study of Health Goals Priority Setting. *Health Policy*, *66*(1), 95–106. https://doi.org/10.1016/S0168-8510(03)00048-4

Abelson, J., Forest, P.-G., Eyles, J. et al. (2003). Deliberations about Deliberative Methods: Issues in the Design and Evaluation of Public Participation Processes. *Social Science & Medicine*, *57*(2), 239–251. https://doi.org/10.1016/S0277-9536(02)00343-X

Abraham, C. (2005, April 9). No Faith in Science. *The Globe and Mail*, F1.

Abramson, M. A., & Lawrence, P. R. (Eds.). (2001). *Transforming Organizations*. Rowman & Littlefield.

American Public Health Association. (2004). *Threats to Public Health Science* (Policy Number 200411). www.apha.org/policies-and-advocacy/public-health-policy-statements/policy-database/2014/07/02/08/52/threats-to-public-health-science

Armenakis, A. A., & Bedeian, A. G. (1999). Organizational Change: A Review of Theory and Research in the 1990s. *Journal of Management*, *25*(3), 293–315. https://doi.org/10.1177/014920639902500303

Aron, J. B. (1982). The Reorganization Syndrome: The Nuclear Regulatory Case. *Southern Review of Public Administration*, *5*(4), 459–476.

Arrow, K. J. (1974). *The Limits of Organization*. Norton.

Ashkenas, R., Ulrich, D., Jick, T., & Kerr, S. (2002). *The Boundaryless Organization: Breaking the Chains of Organizational Structure* (2nd ed.). Jossey-Bass.

Australia Department of Health and Ageing. (2003). *Corporate Plan: Better Health, Better Care, Better Life, 2003–05*. Performance Section, Portfolio Strategies Division, Department of Health and Ageing, Commonwealth of Australia.

Badawy, M. K. (1995). *Developing Managerial Skills in Engineers and Scientists: Succeeding as a Technical Manager* (2nd ed.). Wiley.

Baker, E. L., & Koplan, J. P. (2002). Strengthening the Nation's Public Health Infrastructure: Historic Challenge, Unprecedented Opportunity. *Health Affairs*, *21*(6), 15–27. https://doi.org/10.1377/hlthaff.21.6.15

Baker, E. L., Melton, R. J., Stange, P. V. et al. (1994). Health Reform and the Health of the Public: Forging Community Health Partnerships. *JAMA*, *272*(16), 1276–1282.

Baumgartner, F. R., & Jones, B. D. (1993). *Agendas and Instability in American Politics*. University of Chicago Press.

Becker, M. C. (2004). Organizational Routines: A Review of the Literature. *Industrial and Corporate Change, 13*(4), 643–678. https://doi.org/10.1093/icc/dth026

Bellante, D., & Link, A. N. (1981). Are Public Sector Workers More Risk Averse than Private Sector Workers? *ILR Review, 34*(3), 408–412. https://doi.org/10.1177/001979398103400307

Benedetto, R. F. (1985). *Matrix Management: Theory in Practice*. Kendall/Hunt.

Berkowitz, B., Nicola, R. M., Lafronza, V., & Bekemeier, B. (2005). Turning Point's Legacy. *Journal of Public Health Management and Practice, 11*(2), 97–100. https://journals.lww.com/jphmp/Fulltext/2005/03000/Turning_Point_s_Legacy.1.aspx

Bernheim, B. D., & Whinston, M. D. (1986). Common Agency. *Econometrica, 54*(4), 923. https://doi.org/10.2307/1912844

Bertelli, A. M. (2006a). Delegating to the Quango: Ex Ante and Ex Post Ministerial Constraints. *Governance, 19*(2), 229–249. https://doi.org/10.1111/j.1468-0491.2006.00313.x

Bertelli, A. M. (2006b). Governing the Quango: An Auditing and Cheating Model of Quasi-Governmental Authorities. *Journal of Public Administration Research and Theory, 16*(2), 239–261. https://doi.org/10.1093/jopart/mui047

Birkland, T. A. (1997). *After Disaster: Agenda Setting, Public Policy, and Focusing Events*. Georgetown University Press.

Bowen, M. (2008). *Censoring Science: Inside the Political Attack on Dr. James Hansen and the Truth of Global Warming*. Dutton.

Boyle, J. M. (1979). Reorganization Reconsidered: An Empirical Approach to the Departmentalization Problem. *Public Administration Review, 39*(5), 458. https://doi.org/10.2307/3109920

Brante, T. (1988). Sociological Approaches to the Professions. *Acta Sociologica, 31*(2), 119–142. https://doi.org/10.1177/000169938803100202

Brickley, J. A., Smith, C. W., & Zimmerman, J. L. (2004). *Managerial Economics and Organizational Architecture* (3rd ed.). McGraw-Hill/Irwin.

Buchanan, D. A., Addicott, R., Fitzgerald, L., Ferlie, E., & Baeza, J. I. (2007). Nobody in Charge: Distributed Change Agency in Healthcare. *Human Relations, 60*(7), 1065–1090. https://doi.org/10.1177/0018726707081158

Burns, T., & Stalker, G. M. (1994). *The Management of Innovation* (Rev. ed.). Oxford University Press.

Carpenter, D. P. (2001). *The Forging of Bureaucratic Autonomy: Reputations, Networks, and Policy Innovation in Executive Agencies, 1862–1928*. Princeton University Press.

Carpenter, D. P. (2010). *Reputation and Power: Organizational Image and Pharmaceutical Regulation at the FDA*. Princeton University Press.

Carr-Saunders, A. M., & Wilson, P. A. (1933). *The Professions*. The Clarendon Press.

Carter, J. (2019, August 5). *Government Scientists Are Censoring Themselves*. Scientific American: Observations. https://blogs.scientificamerican.com/observations/government-scientists-are-censoring-themselves/

Carver, G. (2005). *An Overview: Centers for Public Health Preparedness Annual Meeting*. Centers for Disease Control and Prevention.

Centers for Disease Control and Prevention. (2003). *The State of the CDC, Fiscal Year 2003*. www.cdc.gov/about/pdf/resources/socdc2003.pdf

Centers for Disease Control and Prevention. (2004a). *CDC: Protecting Health for Life, the State of the CDC, Fiscal Year 2004*. www.cdc.gov/CDC.pdf

Centers for Disease Control and Prevention. (2004b). *CDC Announces New Goals and Organizational Design*. www.cdc.gov/media/pressrel/r040513.htm

Centers for Disease Control and Prevention. (2005). *Office of Strategy and Innovation*. Centers for Disease Control and Prevention.

Centers for Disease Control and Prevention. (2014, August 1). *The Threat*. Centers for Disease Control and Prevention. www.cdc.gov/anthrax/bioterrorism/threat.html

Centers for Disease Control and Prevention, Agency for Toxic Substances and Disease Registry. (2004). *Report of the Public Health Research Workgroup of the CDC/ATSDR Futures Initiative*. Centers for Disease Control and Prevention, Health Promotion and Education. (2004). *A Report of the Ad Hoc Committee: The Recommendation to Establish a Health Promotion Focal Point within the Centers for Disease Control and Prevention (CDC)*.

Chandler, A. D. (1990). *Strategy and Structure: Chapters in the History of the Industrial Enterprise*. MIT Press.

Christensen, T., & Lægreid, P. (2007). The Whole-of-Government Approach to Public Sector Reform. *Public Administration Review*, *67*(6), 1059–1066. https://doi.org/10.1111/j.1540-6210.2007.00797.x

Coates, D. (2019). *Worldwide Threat Assessment of the United States Intelligence Community*. Director of National Intelligence.

Coleman, P. (2021, October 18). Launching a New Pilot: Government-Wide "Federal Employee Voice" Pulse Surveys. *Performance.Gov*. www.performance.gov/blog/governmentwide-pulse-survey/

Commission of the European Communities. (2007). *Together for Health: A Strategic Approach for the EU 2008–2013*. https://ec.europa.eu/health/archive/ph_overview/documents/strategy_wp_en.pdf

Crow, M. M., & Bozeman, B. (1998). *Limited by Design: R&D Laboratories in the U.S. National Innovation System*. Columbia University Press.

Currie, G., Lockett, A., Finn, R., Martin, G., & Waring, J. (2012). Institutional Work to Maintain Professional Power: Recreating the Model of Medical Professionalism. *Organization Studies*, *33*(7), 937–962. https://doi.org/10.1177/0170840612445116

Cyert, R. M., & March, J. G. (1992). *A Behavioral Theory of the Firm* (2nd ed.). Wiley-Blackwell.

Daft, R. L. (2007). *Organization Theory and Design* (9th ed.). Thomson South-Western.

Dart, B. (2007, March 10). Gerberding "Deeply Concerned" about CDC Morale. *Atlanta Journal-Constitution*, 1A.

Davies, H. T. O. (2003). Trends in Doctor-manager Relationships. *BMJ*, *326*(7390), 646–649. https://doi.org/10.1136/bmj.326.7390.646

Davis, R. M. (1998). "Healthy People 2010": National Health Objectives for the United States. *BMJ*, *317*(7171), 1513–1517. https://doi.org/10.1136/bmj.317.7171.1513

Davis, S. M., & Lawrence, P. R. (1977). *Matrix*. Addison-Wesley.

Davis, S. M., & Lawrence, P. R. (1978). Problems of Matrix Organizations. *Harvard Business Review*, *56*(3), 131–142.

Decker, R. S. (2018). *Recounting the Anthrax Attacks: Terror, the Amerithrax Task Force, and the Evolution of Forensics in the FBI*. Rowman & Littlefield.

Duffy, J. (1990). *The Sanitarians: A History of American Public Health*. University of Illinois Press.

Elster, J. (Ed.). (1998). *Deliberative Democracy*. Cambridge University Press.

Emmerich, H. (1971). *Federal Organization and Administrative Management*. University of Alabama Press.

Etheridge, E. W. (1992). *Sentinel for Health: A History of the Centers for Disease Control*. University of California Press.

European Centre for Disease Prevention and Control. (2005). *Programme of Work for 2005–2006* (Document MB2/9). www.ecdc.europa.eu/sites/default/files/media/en/aboutus/Key%20Documents/05–06_KD_Annual_work_programme.pdf

Evans, P., & Wolf, B. (2005). Collaboration Rules. *Harvard Business Review*, *83*(7), 96–104.

Fauci, A. S. (2017, February 9). What Three Decades Of Pandemic Threats Can Teach Us About The Future. *Health Affairs Blog*. www.healthaffairs.org/do/10.1377/hblog20170209.058678/full/

Feldman, M. S. (2000). Organizational Routines as a Source of Continuous Change. *Organization Science*, *11*(6), 611–629. https://doi.org/10.1287/orsc.11.6.611.12529

Feng, Z., Li, W., & Varma, J. K. (2011). Gaps Remain In China's Ability To Detect Emerging Infectious Diseases Despite Advances Since The Onset Of SARS And Avian Flu. *Health Affairs*, *30*(1), 127–135. https://doi.org/10.1377/hlthaff.2010.0606

Fernandez, S., & Rainey, H. G. (2006). Managing Successful Organizational Change in the Public Sector. *Public Administration Review*, *66*(2), 168–176. https://doi.org/10.1111/j.1540-6210.2006.00570.x

Fletcher, D. S., & Taplin, I. M. (2002). *Understanding Organizational Evolution: Its Impact on Management and Performance*. Quorum Books.

Foege, W. H. (2006). CDC's 60th Anniversary: Director's Perspective – William H. Foege, M. D., M. P. H., 1977–1983. *MMWR Weekly*, *55*(39), 1971–1074.

Forbes, T., Hallier, J., & Kelly, L. (2004). Doctors as Managers: Investors and Reluctants in a Dual Role. *Health Services Management Research*, *17*(3), 167–176. https://doi.org/10.1258/0951484041485638

Freidson, E. (2001). *Professionalism: The Third Logic* (reprint). Polity Press.

Frieden, T., Koplan, J. P., Satcher, D., & Besser, R. (2020, July 14). We Ran the CDC. No President Ever Politicized its Science the Way Trump Has. *Washington Post*. www.washingtonpost.com/outlook/2020/07/14/cdc-directors-trump-politics/

Gailmard, S., & Patty, J. W. (2007). Slackers and Zealots: Civil Service, Policy Discretion, and Bureaucratic Expertise. *American Journal of Political Science*, *51*(4), 873–889. https://doi.org/10.1111/j.1540-5907.2007.00286.x

Galbraith, J. R. (1974). Organization Design: An Information Processing View. *Interfaces*, *4*(3), 28–36. https://doi.org/10.1287/inte.4.3.28

Ghemawat, P. (2003). The Forgotten Strategy. *Harvard Business Review*, *81*(11), 76–84.

Glaser, B. G. (1964). *Organizational Scientists: Their Professional Careers*. Bobbs-Merrill Company. https://books.google.com/books?id=0jJ8AAAAIAAJ

Goggin, W. C. (1974). How the Multidimensional Structure Works and Dow Corning. *Harvard Business Review*, *52*(1), 54–65.

Goodsell, C. T. (2004). *The Case for Bureaucracy: A Public Administration Polemic*. CQ Press.

Gorman, C., & Fulton, G. (2006, November 27). What Ails the CDC. *Time, 168* (22), 60.

Gortner, H. F., Mahler, J., & Nicholson, J. B. (1997). *Organization Theory: A Public Perspective* (2nd ed.). Harcourt Brace College Publishers.

Gottlieb, S. (2021). *Uncontrolled Spread: Why COVID-19 Defeated Us and How We Can Beat the Next Pandemic*. HarperCollins Publishers.

Habermas, J. (1995). Reconciliation Through the Public use of Reason: Remarks on John Rawls's Political Liberalism. *The Journal of Philosophy, 92*(3), 109. https://doi.org/10.2307/2940842

Hall, R. H. (1968). Professionalization and Bureaucratization. *American Sociological Review, 33*(1), 92. https://doi.org/10.2307/2092242

Hammond, T. H. (1986). Agenda Control, Organizational Structure, and Bureaucratic Politics. *American Journal of Political Science, 30*(2), 379. https://doi.org/10.2307/2111102

Hammond, T. H. (1994). Structure, Strategy, and the Agenda of the Firm. In R. Rumelt, D. E. Schendel, & D. J. Teece (Eds.), *Fundamental Issues in Strategy: A Research Agenda.* (pp. 97–154). Harvard Business School Press.

Hammond, T. H., & Thomas, P. A. (1989). The Impossibility of a Neutral Hierarchy. *Journal of Law, Economics, and Organization, 5*(1), 155–184.

Hanson, R., Margolis, J., Levin, M. R., & Letwin, W. (1974). *Reform as Reorganization*. Routledge.

Harrell, J. (2004, September 7). National Institute for Occupational Safety and Health Reorganization under Way. *The Daily Reporter.*

Harris, G. (2006, September 17). Inner Circle Taking More of CDC Bonuses, Agency Record Shows. *New York Times.*

Harris, G. (2010, March 15). Obama's C.D.C. Director, Wielding a Big Broom. *New York Times.*

Hatch, M. J. (2018). *Organization Theory: Modern, Symbolic, and Postmodern Perspectives* (4th ed.). Oxford University Press.

Hirschman, A. O. (1970). *Exit, Voice, and Loyalty: Responses to Decline in Firms, Organizations, and States*. Harvard University Press.

Howlett, M. (2009). Policy Analytical Capacity and Evidence-based Policy-making: Lessons from Canada. *Canadian Public Administration, 52* (2), 153–175. https://doi.org/10.1111/j.1754-7121.2009.00070_1.x

Hult, K. M. (1987). *Agency Merger and Bureaucratic Redesign*. University of Pittsburgh Press.

Hunter, D. J. (1992). Doctors as Managers: Poachers Turned Gamekeepers? *Social Science & Medicine*, *35*(4), 557–566. https://doi.org/10.1016/0277-9536(92)90349-U

Inside OSHA. (2004a, May 31). CDC Regrouping Prompts Concern NIOSH May Lose Power, Shift Focus. *Inside OSHA*, *11*(11).

Inside OSHA. (2004b, July 26). ASSE: Shift NIOSH to Labor Dept. If CDC Reorg Issues Not Resolved. *Inside OSHA*, *11*(15).

Inside OSHA. (2004c, August 23). CDC Director Tells Stakeholders NIOSH Budget to Increase. *Inside OSHA*, *11*(17).

Inside OSHA. (2004d, September 6). CDC Director Modifies Reorganization Effort, Shows Support for NIOSH. *Inside OSHA*, *11*(18).

Inside OSHA. (2004e, September 20). Senate Appropriators Tell CDC to Leave Current NIOSH Structure Intact. *Inside OSHA*, *11*(19).

Inside OSHA. (2004f). Senate Appropriators may Criticize CDC for Proceeding with NIOSH Restructuring. *Inside OSHA*, *11*(22).

Inside OSHA. (2004g, November 29). Congress Votes to Instruct CDC to Exclude NIOSH from Reorg Effort. *Inside OSHA*, *11*(24).

Inside OSHA. (2004h, December 13). CDC to Abide by Congress' Call to Reverse Structural Changes to NIOSH. *Inside OSHA*, *11*(25).

Inside OSHA. (2005a, April 4). AIHA, ASSE Urge Lawmakers to Consider Shifting NIOSH to DOL. *Inside OSHA*, *12*(7).

Inside OSHA. (2005b, May 16). Stakeholders Still Concerned over NIOSH's Role in CDC. *Inside OSHA*, *12*(10).

Isabella, L. A. (1990). Evolving Interpretations as a Change Unfolds: How Managers Construe Key Organizational Events. *Academy of Management Journal*, *33*(1), 7–41. https://doi.org/10.5465/256350

Jones, B. D., & Baumgartner, F. R. (2005). *The Politics of Attention: How Government Prioritizes Problems*. University of Chicago Press.

Jones, C., Hesterly, W. S., & Borgatti, S. P. (1997). A General Theory of Network Governance: Exchange Conditions and Social Mechanisms. *The Academy of Management Review*, *22*(4), 911. https://doi.org/10.2307/259249

Jones, G. R. (2004). *Organizational Theory, Design, and Change: Text and Cases* (4th ed.). Pearson Prentice Hall.

Kerr, S., Von Glinow, M. A., & Schriesheim, J. (1977). Issues in the Study of "Professionals" in Organizations: The Case of Scientists and Engineers. *Organizational Behavior and Human Performance*, *18*(2), 329–345. https://doi.org/10.1016/0030-5073(77)90034-4

Kettl, D. F. (2005). *The Next Government of the United States: Challenges for Performance in the 21st Century*. IBM Center for the Business of

Government. www.businessofgovernment.org/report/next-government-united-states-challenges-performance-21st-century

Kettl, D. F. (2007). *Reflections on 21st Century Government Management*. IBM Center for the Business of Government. www.businessofgovernment.org/sites/default/files/KettlKelmanReport.pdf

Kettl, D. F. (2021). *Politics of the Administrative Process* (Eighth edition). SAGE/CQ Press.

Knight, J. (1992). *Institutions and Social Conflict*. Cambridge University Press.

Knight, J., & Johnson, J. (1994). Aggregation and Deliberation: On the Possibility of Democratic Legitimacy. *Political Theory*, *22*(2), 277–296. https://doi.org/10.1177/0090591794022002004

Kotter, J. P. (2012). *Leading Change*. Harvard Business Review Press.

Krakauer, D. (2020, March 30). By Using Transmission to our Advantage, We can Eliminate Coronavirus through Citizen-based Medicine. *Santa Fe Institute Transmission: Complexity Science for COVID-19*. https://sfi-edu .s3.amazonaws.com/sfi-edu/production/uploads/ckeditor/2020/04/05/t-000-krakauer_Cuf31X9.pdf

Lan, L. (2005). Open Government and Transparent Policy: China's Experiences with SARS. *International Public Management Review*, *6*(1), 60–75.

Larson, E. W., & Gobeli, D. H. (1987). Matrix Management: Contradictions and Insights. *California Management Review*, *29*(4), 126–138. https://doi.org/10.2307/41162135

Larson, E. W., & Gobeli, D. H. (1988). Organizing for Product Development Projects. *Journal of Product Innovation Management*, *5*(3), 180–190. https://doi.org/10.1111/1540-5885.530180

Latham, G. P., & Yukl, G. A. (1975). A Review of Research on the Application of Goal Setting in Organizations. *Academy of Management Journal*, *18*(4), 824–845. https://doi.org/10.2307/255381

Lee, S.-Y., & Whitford, A. B. (2007). Exit, Voice, Loyalty, and Pay: Evidence from the Public Workforce. *Journal of Public Administration Research and Theory*, *18*(4), 647–671. https://doi.org/10.1093/jopart/mum029

Lee, S.-Y., Yun, T., Whitford, A. B., & Lim, J. Y. (2020). The Reorganization of the US Citizenship and Immigration Services (USCIS) and Its Effects. *Public Organization Review*, *20*(4), 647–663. https://doi.org/10.1007/s11115-019-00462-4

Lewis, D. E. (2003). *Presidents and the Politics of Agency Design: Political Insulation in the United States Government Bureaucracy, 1946–1997*. Stanford University Press.

Lewis, M. (2021). *The Premonition: A Pandemic Story* (First Edition). W.W. Norton & Company.

Li, C., Sun, M., Wang, Y. et al. (2016). The Centers for Disease Control and Prevention System in China: Trends From 2002–2012. *American Journal of Public Health*, *106*(12), 2093–2102. https://doi.org/10.2105/AJPH.2016.303508

Lipton, E., Goodnough, A., Shear, M. D. et al. (2020, June 3). The C.D.C. Waited "Its Entire Existence for This Moment." What Went Wrong? *New York Times*. www.nytimes.com/2020/06/03/us/cdc-coronavirus.html

Locke, E. A., Latham, G. P., & Erez, M. (1988). The Determinants of Goal Commitment. *The Academy of Management Review*, *13*(1), 23. https://doi.org/10.2307/258352

Lohr, S. (2002, January 1). 2 Computer Giants Hope to Avoid Pitfalls of Past Mergers. *The New York Times*, 1.

Majone, G. (1989). *Evidence, Argument, and Persuasion in the Policy Process*. Yale University Press.

Majone, G. (2006). Agenda Setting. In M. Moran, M. Rein, & R. F. Goodin (Eds.), *The Oxford Handbook of Public Policy*. (pp. 228–250). Oxford University Press.

March, J. G., & Olson, J. P. (1983). Organizing Political Life: What Administrative Reorganization Tells Us about Government. *American Political Science Review*, *77*(2), 281–296. https://doi.org/10.2307/1958916

March, J. G., & Romelaer, P. (1976). Position and Presence in the Drift of Decisions. In J. G. March and J. P. Olson (Eds.) *Ambiguity and Choice in Organizations* (pp. 251–276). Universitetsforlaget.

March, J. G., Schulz, M., & Chou, H. (2000). *The Dynamics of Rules: Change in Written Organizational Codes*. Stanford University Press.

March, J. G., Simon, H. A., & Guetzkow, H. S. (1993). *Organizations* (2nd ed.). Blackwell.

Mason, K. A. (2016). *Infectious Change: Reinventing Chinese Public Health after an Epidemic*. Stanford University Press.

Maxmen, A., & Tollefson, J. (2020, August 4). *Two Decades of Pandemic War Games Failed to Account for Donald Trump*. Nature. www.nature.com/articles/d41586-020-02277-6

Maynard-Moody, S., Stull, D. D., & Mitchell, J. (1986). Reorganization as Status Drama: Building, Maintaining, and Displacing Dominant Subcultures. *Public Administration Review*, *46*(4), 301. https://doi.org/10.2307/976303

McCormick, J. B., Fisher-Hoch, S., & Horvitz, L. A. (1999). *Level 4: Virus Hunters of the CDC – Tracking Ebola and the World's Deadliest Viruses*. Sterling.

McDowell, D. (2005, September 21). *A New Look at Networking in the 21st Century*. 13th Annual Public Health Distance Learning Summit "New Horizons in Distance Learning for Public Health", CDC, Global Communications Center, Atlanta, GA.

McKenna, M. A. J. (2004, April 20). CDC to Change Structure Slightly. *Atlanta Journal-Constitution*, 5A.

Meagher, K. J. (2003). Generalizing Incentives and Loss of Control in an Optimal Hierarchy: The Role of Information Technology. *Economics Letters*, *78*(2), 273–280. https://doi.org/10.1016/S0165-1765(02)00220-3

Meier, K. J. (1980). Executive Reorganization of Government: Impact on Employment and Expenditures. *American Journal of Political Science*, *24*(3), 396. https://doi.org/10.2307/2110825

Meier, R. L. (1951). Research as a Social Process: Social Status, Specialism, and Technological Advance in Great Britain. *The British Journal of Sociology*, *2*(2), 91. https://doi.org/10.2307/587381

Merton, R. K. (1957). Priorities in Scientific Discovery: A Chapter in the Sociology of Science. *American Sociological Review*, *22*(6), 635. https://doi.org/10.2307/2089193

Miller, G. J. (1992). *Managerial Dilemmas: The Political Economy of Hierarchy*. Cambridge University Press.

Miller, G. J., & Whitford, A. B. (2016). *Above Politics: Bureaucratic Discretion and Credible Commitment*. Cambridge University Press.

Milne, T. L. (2000). Strengthening Local Public Health Practice: A View to the Millennium: *Journal of Public Health Management and Practice*, *6*(1), 61–66. https://doi.org/10.1097/00124784-200006010-00010

Mintzberg, H. (1979). *The Structuring of Organizations: A Synthesis of the Research*. Prentice-Hall.

Moe, R. C. (1991). The HUD Scandal and the Case for an Office of Federal Management. *Public Administration Review*, *51*(4), 298. https://doi.org/10.2307/976745

Moe, T. M. (1987). Interests, Institutions, and Positive Theory: The Politics of the NLRB. *Studies in American Political Development*, *2*, 236–299. https://doi.org/10.1017/S0898588X00001784

Moe, T. M. (1989). The Politics of Bureaucratic Structure. In J. E. Chubb & P. E. Peterson (Eds.), *Can the Government Govern?* (pp. 267–329). The Brookings Institution.

Morens, D. M., Folkers, G. K., & Fauci, A. S. (2008). Emerging Infections: A Perpetual Challenge. *The Lancet Infectious Diseases*, *8*(11), 710–719. https://doi.org/10.1016/S1473-3099(08)70256-1

Mosher, F. C. (1967). *Governmental Reorganizations: Cases and Commentary*. Bobbs-Merrill Company.

Nelson, R. R., & Winter, S. G. (1982). *An Evolutionary Theory of Economic Change*. Belknap Press of Harvard University Press.

Neslund, V., Lisco, J. D., Dietz, S. E. et al. (2004, November 6). *CDC's Futures Initiative: CDC's Employees, Public Health Customers, Partners, and Channels*. American Public Health Association, 2004. https://apha.confex .com/apha/132am/techprogram/paper_86568.htm

Nesmith, J. (2006, September 28). Scientists to Take on White House: Group Objects to "Political Assault" on Research Issues. *Cox News Service Washington Bureau*.

Nesmith, J. (2007, April 4). Politics Called Threat to CDC; Ex-Directors Say Integrity, Morale at Risk. *Atlanta Journal-Constitution*, 5A.

Nesmith, J., & Young, A. (2007, February 23). Caucus Seek "Up-close Under-standing" of CDC. *Atlanta Journal-Constitution*.

Nicholson-Crotty, S., Nicholson-Crotty, J., & Fernandez, S. (2017). Performance and Management in the Public Sector: Testing a Model of Relative Risk Aversion. *Public Administration Review*, *77*(4), 603–614. https://doi.org/ 10.1111/puar.12619

North, D. C. (1990). *Institutions, Institutional Change, and Economic Performance*. Cambridge University Press.

Parsons, T. (1939). The Professions and Social Structure. *Social Forces*, *17*(4), 457–467. https://doi.org/10.2307/2570695

Perrow, C. (1961). The Analysis of Goals in Complex Organizations. *American Sociological Review*, *26*(6), 854. https://doi.org/10.2307/2090570

Peters, B. G. (1992). Government Reorganization: A Theoretical Analysis. *International Political Science Review*, *13*(2), 199–217. https://doi.org/ 10.1177/019251219201300204

Pfeifer, C. (2011). Risk Aversion and Sorting into Public Sector Employment. *German Economic Review*, *12*(1), 85–99. https://doi.org/10.1111/j.1468-0475.2010.00505.x

Pfiffner, J. P. (2007). The First MBA President: George W. Bush as Public Administrator. *Public Administration Review*, *67*(1), 6–20. https://doi.org/ 10.1111/j.1540-6210.2006.00691.x

Powley, E. H., & Piderit, S. K. (2008). Tending Wounds: Elements of the Organizational Healing Process. *The Journal of Applied Behavioral Science*, *44*(1), 134–149. https://doi.org/10.1177/0021886308314842

Public Health Agency of Canada. (2005a). *2005–2006 Report on Plans and Priorities*. www.canada.ca/en/public-health/corporate/transparency/corpor ate-management-reporting/reports-plans-priorities.html

Public Health Agency of Canada. (2005b). *Integrated Pan-Canadian Healthy Living Strategy*. www.canada.ca/en/public-health/services/ health-promotion/healthy-living/2005-integrated-canadian-healthy-liv ing-strategy.html

Public Health Service, Office of the Assistant Secretary for Health and Surgeon General, U.S. Department of Health, Education, and Welfare. (1979). *Healthy People: The Surgeon General's Report on Health Promotion and Disease Prevention*. U.S. Government Printing Office. https://profiles.nlm.nih.gov/spotlight/nn/catalog/nlm:nlmuid-101584932X94-doc

Public Health Service, U.S. Department of Health and Human Services. (1980). *Promoting Health/Preventing Disease: Objectives for the Nation*. https://stacks.cdc.gov/view/cdc/5293

Public Health Service, U.S. Department of Health and Human Services. (1991). *Healthy People 2000: National Health Promotion and Disease Prevention Objectives*. www.cdc.gov/nchs/data/hp2000/hp2k01.pdf

Radin, B. A. (2007). The Instruments of Intergovernmental Management. In B. G. Peters & J. Pierre (Eds.), *The Sage Handbook of Public Administration*. (pp.735–749) Sage.

Raelin, J. A. (1991). *The Clash of Cultures: Managers Managing Professionals*. Harvard Business School Press.

Rainey, H. G., & Thompson, J. (2006). Leadership and the Transformation of a Major Institution: Charles Rossotti and the Internal Revenue Service. *Public Administration Review, 66*(4), 596–604. https://doi.org/10.1111/j.1540-6210.2006.00619.x

Ren, X., Wang, L., Cowling, B. J. et al. (2019). Systematic Review: National Notifiable Infectious Disease Surveillance System in China. *Online Journal of Public Health Informatics, 11*(1). https://doi.org/10.5210/ojphi.v11i1.9897

Robertson, P. J., & Seneviratne, S. J. (1995). Outcomes of Planned Organizational Change in the Public Sector: A Meta-Analytic Comparison to the Private Sector. *Public Administration Review, 55*(6), 547. https://doi.org/10.2307/3110346

Sabatier, P. A. (1988). An Advocacy Coalition Framework of Policy Change and the Role of Policy-oriented Learning Therein. *Policy Sciences, 21*(2–3), 129–168. https://doi.org/10.1007/BF00136406

Salamon, L. M. (1981). The Question of Goals. In P. Szanton (Ed.), *Federal Reorganization: What Have We Learned?* (pp.58–84). Chatham House.

Sapienza, A. M. (2004). *Managing Scientists: Leadership Strategies in Scientific Research* (2nd ed.). Wiley-Liss.

Sayles, L. R., & Chandler, M. K. (1971). *Managing Large Systems: Organizations for the Future*. Harper and Row.

Shoop, T. (2007, March 1). Winning Over the Workers [National Journal Group]. *GovExec.Com*. www.govexec.com/magazine-advice-and-dissent/

magazine-advice-and-dissent-outlook/2007/03/winning-over-the-workers/23846/

Simon, H. A. (1964). On the Concept of Organizational Goal. *Administrative Science Quarterly, 9*(1), 1. https://doi.org/10.2307/2391519

Sinclair, A. H., & Whitford, A. B. (2013). Separation and Integration in Public Health: Evidence from Organizational Structure in the States. *Journal of Public Administration Research and Theory, 23*(1), 55–77. https://doi.org/10.1093/jopart/mus005

Sinclair, A. H., & Whitford, A. B. (2015). Effects of Participation and Collaboration on Perceived Effectiveness of Core Public Health Functions. *American Journal of Public Health, 105*(8), 1638–1645. https://doi.org/10.2105/AJPH.2015.302586

Slavitt, A. (2021). *Preventable: The Inside Story of How Leadership Failures, Politics, and Selfishness Doomed the U.S. Coronavirus Response*. Macmillan.

Smith, B. L. R. (1992). *The Advisers: Scientists in the Policy Process*. Brookings Institution.

Stein, R. (2005, March 6). Internal Dissension as the CDC Faces Big Threats to Public Health. *Washington Post*, A09.

Sun, L. H. (2018, May 10). Top White House Official in Charge of Pandemic Response Exits Abruptly. *Washington Post*. www.washingtonpost.com/news/to-your-health/wp/2018/05/10/top-white-house-official-in-charge-of-pandemic-response-exits-abruptly/

Surowiecki, J. (2004). *The Wisdom of Crowds: Why the Many are Smarter than the Few and How Collective Wisdom Shapes Business, Economies, Societies, and Nations* (1st ed.). Doubleday.

Sydow, J., Schreyögg, G., & Koch, J. (2009). Organizational Path Dependence: Opening the Black Box. *Academy of Management Review, 34*(4), 689–709. https://doi.org/10.5465/amr.34.4.zok689

Taleb, N. N. (2007). *The Black Swan: The Impact of the Highly Improbable* (1st ed.). Random House.

Tarkowski, Z. M. T., & Turnbull, A. V. (1959). Scientists Versus Administrators: An Approach Towards Archieving Greater Understanding. *Public Administration, 37*(3), 213–256. https://doi.org/10.1111/j.1467-9299.1959.tb01540.x

Taubenberger, J. K., Morens, D. M., & Fauci, A. S. (2007). The Next Influenza Pandemic: Can It Be Predicted? *JAMA, 297*(18), 2025. https://doi.org/10.1001/jama.297.18.2025

Taylor, A. (1999, August 16). Compaq Looks Inside for Salvation. *Fortune*, 126.

Taylor, B. (1991). The Logic of Global Business: An Interview with ABB's Percy Barnevik. *Harvard Business Review, 69*(2), 90–105.

Temples, J. R. (1982). The Nuclear Regulatory Commission and the Politics of Regulatory Reform: Since Three Mile Island. *Public Administration Review, 42*(4), 355. https://doi.org/10.2307/975979

Thomas, C. W. (1993). Reorganizing Public Organizations: Alternatives, Objectives, and Evidence. *Journal of Public Administration Research and Theory,3*(4), 457–486. https://doi.org/10.1093/oxfordjournals.jpart.a037181

Thompson, G. (2003). *Between Hierarchies and Markets: The Logic and Limits of Network Forms of Organization.* Oxford University Press.

Thompson, J. D., & McEwen, W. J. (1958). Organizational Goals and Environment: Goal-Setting as an Interaction Process. *American Sociological Review, 23*(1), 23. https://doi.org/10.2307/2088620

Travers, J., & Milgram, S. (1977). An Experimental Study of the Small World Problem. In S. Leinhardt (Ed.), *Social Networks (pp.* 179–197). Elsevier. https://doi.org/10.1016/B978-0-12-442450-0.50018-3

United Kingdom Department of Health and Social Care. (1999). *Saving Lives: Our Healthier Nation.* The Stationary Office. https://assets.publishing.service.gov.uk/government/uploads/system/uploads/attachment_data/file/265576/4386.pdf

United Kingdom Health Protection Agency. (2004). *Health Protection Agency Corporate Plan 2004/2009.* HPA, United Kingdom.

United States Institute of Medicine (Ed.). (1988). *The Future of Public Health.* National Academy Press.

United States Institute of Medicine (Ed.). (2003). *The future of the Public's Health in the 21st Century.* National Academies Press.

United States Senate Subcommittee on Federal Financial Management, Government Information, and International Security, Minority Office. (2007). *CDC Off Center: A Review of How an Agency Tasked with Fighting and Preventing Disease has Spent Hundreds of Millions of Tax Dollars for Failed Prevention Efforts, International Junkets, and Lavish Facilities, but Cannot Demonstrate It is Controlling Disease.* www.cbsnews.com/htdocs/pdf/cdc_off_center.pdf

U.S. Centers for Disease Control and Prevention. (2005). *CDC at Work Today! Best Business Practices.* www.cdc.gov/media/pressrel/r050421a.htm

U.S. Department of Health and Human Services. (2011). *Healthy People 2010.* U.S. Government Printing Office. www.cdc.gov/nchs/healthy_people/hp2010/hp2010_final_review.htm

U.S. Department of Health and Human Services. (2015, February 2). *HHS FY2016 Budget in Brief.* www.hhs.gov/about/budget/budget-in-brief/cdc/

index.html#:~:text=The%20FY%202016%20Budget%20request,Health%20Fund%20(Prevention%20Fund).

U.S. Department of Health and Human Services, Office of Inspector General. (1999). *Audit of Costs Charged to the Chronic Fatigue Syndrome Program at the Centers for Disease Control and Prevention* (A-04–98–04226). https://oig.hhs.gov/oas/reports/region4/49804226.pdf

U.S. Government Accountability Office. (2000a). *West Nile Virus Outbreak: Lessons for Public Health Preparedness* (HEHS-00–180). www.gao.gov/products/HEHS-00-180

U.S. Government Accountability Office. (2000b). *Centers for Disease Control and Prevention: Independent Accountants Identify Financial Management Weaknesses* (GAO-01–40). www.gao.gov/products/GAO-01-40

U.S. Government Accountability Office. (2002). *Homeland Security: CDC's Oversight of the Select Agent Program* (GAO-03-315 R). www.gao.gov/products/GAO-03-315 R

U.S. Government Accountability Office. (2004). *Centers for Disease Control and Prevention: Agency Leadership Taking Steps to Improve Management and Planning, but Challenges Remain* (GAO-04–219). www.gao.gov/products/GAO-04-219

U.S. Office of Personnel Management. (2020, July 28). *Federal Employee Viewpoint Survey.* www.opm.gov/fevs/

Vlieg, W. L., Fanoy, E. B., van Asten, L. et al. (2017). Comparing National Infectious Disease Surveillance Systems: China and the Netherlands. *BMC Public Health, 17*(1), 415. https://doi.org/10.1186/s12889-017-4319-3

Wagner, J. A., Leana, C. R., Locke, E. A., & Schweiger, D. M. (1997). Cognitive and Motivational Frameworks in U.S. Research on Participation: A Meta-analysis of Primary Effects. *Journal of Organizational Behavior, 18*(1), 49–65. https://doi.org/10.1002/(SICI)1099-1379(199701)18:1<49::AID-JOB789>3.0.CO;2-P

Wahlberg, D. (2005, July 26). Morale of the CDC workers Could Use a Booster Shot. *Atlanta Journal-Constitution*, A1.

Wahlberg, D., & McKenna, M. A. J. (2005, February 6). CDC Cuts Could Hurt Bioterror Effort; Bush '06 Budget: De-emphasizing Agency Makes U.S. More Vulnerable, Health Advocates Say. *Atlanta Journal-Constitution*, 3A.

Ward, A. (2006, October 23). Graduate of Duke has a Global View on Hazards. *Financial Times*.

Weible, C. M., & Sabatier, P. A. (2009). Coalitions, Science, and Belief Change: Comparing Adversarial and Collaborative Policy Subsystems. *Policy Studies Journal, 37*(2), 195–212. https://doi.org/10.1111/j.1541-0072.2009.00310.x

Weick, K. E. (1995). *Sensemaking in Organizations.* Sage.

Weiss, R. (2004, August 31). Change at the CDC Draws Protest. *Washington Post*, A19.

Weiss, R. (2005, July 20). Bill Would Give NIH Director Broad Power over Spending. *Washington Post*, A21.

Whetten, D. A. (1987). Organizational Growth and Decline Processes. *Annual Review of Sociology*, *13*(1), 335–358. https://doi.org/10.1146/annurev.so.13.080187.002003

Whitford, A. B. (2006). Unitary, Divisional, And Matrix Forms As Political Governance Systems. *Journal of Management & Governance*, *10*(4), 435–454. https://doi.org/10.1007/s10997-006-9009-y

Whitford, A. B. (2021). Presidential Reorganization and the Politics of Public Agencies. *Administration & Society*, *53*(2), 193–221. https://doi.org/10.1177/0095399720945965

Whitford, A. B., & Lee, S.-Y. (2015). Exit, Voice, and Loyalty with Multiple Exit Options: Evidence from the US Federal Workforce. *Journal of Public Administration Research and Theory*, *25*(2), 373–398. https://doi.org/10.1093/jopart/muu004

Wilensky, H. L. (1964). The Professionalization of Everyone? *American Journal of Sociology*, *70*(2), 137–158. https://doi.org/10.1086/223790

Wilkinson, T. (1998). *Science under Siege: The Politicians' War on Nature and Truth*. Johnson Books.

Williamson, O. E. (1985). *The Economic Institutions of Capitalism: Firms, Markets, Relational Contracting*. Free Press.

Wilson, J. Q. (1989). *Bureaucracy: What Government Agencies Do and Why They Do It*. Basic Books.

Wilson, K. (2018, October 5). *Will Trump Restructure the NIH?* www.ascb.org/science-policy/will-trump-restructure-nih/

Woodhouse, M. (2004, September 20). CDC Reorganization: Groups Say It Diminishes Importance of Workplace Safety. *Atlanta Business Chronicle*.

Young, A. (2006a, May 24). Congress Looks at Allegations of Discord at CDC. *Atlanta Journal-Constitution*, A1.

Young, A. (2006b, September 10). Exodus, Morale Shake CDC. *Atlanta Journal-Constitution*.

Young, A. (2006c, September 17). CDC Will Examine Fairness of Bonuses: Chief Financial Officer, Who has Received Tens of Thousands in Cash Awards Since 2000, Co-chairs a Panel to Examine Rewards Program. *Atlanta Journal-Constitution*, 1A.

Young, A. (2006d, September 17). Science Slighted in CDC Awards; Cash Bonuses at Troubled Health Agency Frequently Go to Bureaucrats Instead of Researchers. *Atlanta Journal-Constitution*, 1A.

Young, A. (2006e, September 21). GAO Joins Inquiry of CDC with 2 Audits. *Atlanta Journal-Constitution*, 3A.

Young, A. (2006f, October 8). CDC Boss: Change had to be Made. *Atlanta Journal-Constitution*, 1A.

Young, A. (2006g, October 25). CDC Overhaul Scrutinized by House Panel; Congress Steps Up Review on Several Fronts. *Atlanta Journal-Constitution*, 3A.

Young, A. (2006h, November 16). Katrina Brought "Chaos" to CDC; Report Criticizes Managers' Response. *Atlanta Journal-Constitution*, 1A.

Young, A. (2006i, December 3). CDC Deal Possibly Unlawful; Internal Review Criticizes How Firm was Picked. *Atlanta Journal-Constitution*, 1A.

Young, A. (2006j, December 8). House Panel Again Seeks CDC Critique. *Atlanta Journal-Constitution*.

Young, A. (2007a, January 22). Report on CDC's Ills Likely Out Today; Ombudsmen Tackle Morale Problems. *Atlanta Journal-Constitution*, 1B.

Young, A. (2007b, January 23). CDC to Hire Full-Time Ombudsmen; Morale Moves: Temporary Consultants' E-mail to Staff Notes Employee Concerns about Matters such as Pay, Workplace Environment. *Atlanta Journal-Constitution*, 1D.

Young, A. (2007c, January 25). Senator Seeks CDC Briefing on Status of Morale Problems. *Atlanta Journal-Constitution*, 3D.

Young, A. (2007d, January 31). CDC Memo Cites Anger, Frustration; Staff Fears "Things Spinning Out of Control," Official Says. *Atlanta Journal-Constitution*, 1A.

Young, A. (2007e, March 24). CDC Rebuffs U.S. Senator; Denial of Briefing Brings Blistering Reply. *Atlanta Journal-Constitution*.

Young, A. (2007f, April 6). Few Fuss in CDC's Morale Inquiry; Out of 14,000, Just 98 Weigh In. *Atlanta Journal-Constitution*, 4A.

Young, A. (2007g, November 1). Key CDC Official Takes Job in Iraq. *Atlanta Journal-Constitution*, 1A.

Yukl, G., Gordon, A., & Taber, T. (2002). A Hierarchical Taxonomy of Leadership Behavior: Integrating a Half Century of Behavior Research. *Journal of Leadership & Organizational Studies*, *9*(1), 15–32. https://doi .org/10.1177/107179190200900102

Cambridge Elements ☰

Public Policy

M. Ramesh
National University of Singapore (NUS)

M. Ramesh is UNESCO Chair on Social Policy Design at the Lee Kuan Yew School of Public Policy, NUS. His research focuses on governance and social policy in East and Southeast Asia, in addition to public policy institutions and processes. He has published extensively in reputed international journals. He is Co-editor of *Policy and Society and Policy Design and Practice.*

Michael Howlett
Simon Fraser University, British Colombia

Michael Howlett is Burnaby Mountain Professor and Canada Research Chair (Tier 1) in the Department of Political Science, Simon Fraser University. He specializes in public policy analysis, and resource and environmental policy. He is currently editor-in-chief of *Policy Sciences* and co-editor of the *Journal of Comparative Policy Analysis, Policy and Society and Policy Design and Practice.*

Xun WU
Hong Kong University of Science and Technology

Xun WU is Professor and Head of the Division of Public Policy at the Hong Kong University of Science and Technology. He is a policy scientist whose research interests include policy innovations, water resource management and health policy reform. He has been involved extensively in consultancy and executive education, his work involving consultations for the World Bank and UNEP.

Judith Clifton
University of Cantabria

Judith Clifton is Professor of Economics at the University of Cantabria, Spain. She has published in leading policy journals and is editor-in-chief of the *Journal of Economic Policy Reform*. Most recently, her research enquires how emerging technologies can transform public administration, a forward-looking cutting-edge project which received €3.5 million funding from the Horizon2020 programme.

Eduardo Araral
National University of Singapore (NUS)

Eduardo Araral is widely published in various journals and books and has presented in forty conferences. He is currently Co-Director of the Institute of Water Policy at the Lee Kuan Yew School of Public Policy, NUS, and is a member of the editorial board of *Journal of Public Administration Research and Theory* and the board of the Public Management Research Association.

About the Series
Elements in Public Policy is a concise and authoritative collection of assessments of the state of the art and future research directions in public policy research, as well as substantive new research on key topics. Edited by leading scholars in the field, the series is an ideal medium for reflecting on and advancing the understanding of critical issues in the public sphere. Collectively, it provides a forum for broad and diverse coverage of all major topics in the field while integrating different disciplinary and methodological approaches.

Cambridge Elements ≡

Public Policy

Elements in the Series

A full series listing is available at: www.cambridge.org/EPPO